PARENTAL GUIDANCE SUGGESTED

A 25-Day Journey to Becoming the Disciple-Maker of Your Home

Dr. Mark Smith

www.parentalguidancesuggested.org

ISBN-13: 978-1-935256-25-0

L'Edge Press
PO Box 1652
Boone, NC 28607
ledgepress.com
ledgepress@gmail.com

Acknowledgments

Dedicated to my biggest fan, my best friend, and my bride, Sherri Smith

Special Thanks

Mark & Tracey Shanks

Greg & Cindy Williams

Jeff & Heather Pope

Doug & Anissa Leatherman

Matt & Valeree Adams

Ryan & Julie Pruett

Matt & Joni Fallaw

Mark & Teresa Killian

Mike & Natalie Owen

George & Pat Council

Matt & Stacey Bolick

Joel & Angie Parker

Kim Crane

Julia Gruver

Beverly DeBonis

Dr. Bill Bennett

Mike Powers

Mark Holmen

Troy Howard

Vicki Gruver

Don Goosman

Cover & Interior Design by Abbie Frease and Abby Smith

When I finished reading Dr. Mark Smith's manuscript I said to myself, this is a great book that weaves together compelling Biblical evidence, great research, and lots of practical advice. I love a book that combines these three things because it serves to both inspire, motivate, and equip us. I strongly recommend this book to parents and church leaders and to Mark I simply say, "Well done good and faithful servant!"
— Pastor Mark Holmen, Author and Missionary to the Faith@Home Movement

Discipleship is the heart of Christianity. Yet few Christians know how to disciple. This book enables every parent to become a discipler.
— Dave & Vicki Gruver, Co-Founders, Christian Family International – Hickory, NC

This book is the perfect blend of challenging Bible study, relevant statistics, and practical ideas on how to truly disciple your child. Mark draws from his years of experience as a student pastor and a parent to prepare you for the next level of focusing your child on Christ. As a parent this book has challenged me with my children and as a youth pastor shaped how I equip parents of teenagers. If you are connected with children or teenagers in any way, this is a must have resource.
— Rev. Mike Powers, Student Pastor, Hickory Grove Baptist Church Main Campus – Charlotte, NC

At last, a book that practically helps parents disciple their children. My friend Dr. Mark Smith has written a resource that will transform your family. This book is a gift to the church and a practical tool for moms and dads who seek to help their children "treasure Christ above all else."
— Steve Wright, Author of ApParent Privilege and reThink.

So many parents today are missing out on the divine blessing that comes from providing spiritual guidance for our children in the home. Dr. Mark Smith has provided a deeply scriptural and practical guide for how parents can help our kids become more passionate followers of Jesus Christ. Every parent who uses Parental Guidance Suggested will find it challenging and beneficial. I praise God for this great resource!
— Dr. Stephen N. Rummage, Senior Pastor, Bell Shoals Baptist Church – Brandon, FL

FOREWORD
Dr. Bill Bennett
President of Mentoring Men for the Master

The Family in America is in deep trouble and facing devastating problems which cry out for an answer. I am, therefore, absolutely ecstatic to recommend to you a book which identifies the problems and presents biblical solutions. The book is designed with three things in mind:

- *To be an easy short read*
- *To give the reader seven days to read five days of material, and*
- *To serve as an individual or small group study for six weeks.*

The book consists of 5 chapters, each of which addresses a specific problem and assigns who is responsible for dealing with the problem:

Chapter 1 – Shows the one essential reason God has put the "precious jewels" of children in the hands of parents to introduce them to His Son, Jesus Christ.

Chapter 2 – Bears the caption, "It All Starts with You," "You" being the parents who must develop holiness to lead their children. One quote summarizes this chapter, "We teach what we know, we reproduce what we are." (John Maxwell)

Chapter 3 – Explores biblical ways parents should lead their families to Jesus Christ as Lord and Savior and into deeper relations with Him.

Chapter 4 – The focus of this chapter is to explicate the time-honored text, but generally misunderstood, of Proverbs 22:6, which calls upon parents to discover the "natural God-given bent of each of their children" and to teach and lead them to fulfill God's purpose for their lives. Three basic ways of learning are explored: Visual, Auditory, and Kinesthetic.

Chapter 5 – This chapter is entitled "Environment of Spiritual Growth." Thus this chapter is about "parents cultivating an environment of spiritual growth in your home."

All the above materials are designed as a Small Group Bible Study for six weeks:

> **Week 1** – Introduction and Distribution of books
> **Week 2** – Discuss week-one reading material
> **Week 3** – Discuss week-two reading material
> **Week 4** – Discuss week three reading material
> **Week 5** – Discuss week four reading material
> **Week 6** – Discuss week five reading material
> **Week 7** – Eat together and share success stories (Optional)

As a pastor for more than 50 years, of churches ranging from 85 to 8000 in membership, I attempted to apprize parents of their God-given responsibility to be "prophet, priest, and King" in their homes and the biblical ways they could accomplish this awesome task. I only wish I had had Dr. Mark Smith's book. But you pastors and parents who read my words know of his book, and I urge you to take advantage of it.

Finally, the most persuasive recommendation of this book is not mine, but the fact that Brother Mark has lived out the Biblical principles he sets forth in his own home and has developed a marvelous family. This I know because I mentored him for several years. I salute Brother Mark for not only sharing his remarkable insights in writing but also for demonstrating himself how his principles, when obeyed, results in a great home. Need I say more except to say you should do five things:

- *Buy the book*
- *Read it*
- *Apply it*
- *Recommend to others*
- *Give it as a gift to your peers.*

Table of Contents

TAG YOU'RE IT

Read This First – Week 1 Intro...

Are there times when you struggle keeping all the plates spinning? Between all the work schedules, appointments, social commitments, homework, and sporting events, sometimes life can feel like it's going in fast motion. When you're being pulled in ten different directions, it's easy to become disconnected from the most precious people God has given us. We can feel we are ineffective as parents and think we have no influence in the lives of our children. If we're not careful, our jobs, obligations, and activities can get in the way of the greatest responsibility we have in life...our family. If any of this sounds remotely familiar, then I'm glad this book is in your hands.

Starting this week, we will begin a journey to discover God's most important assignment for you as a parent. He has placed in your capable hands some precious cargo. He's given you children for many reasons, but there is one essential reason God has put these priceless jewels in your care. He desires for them to be introduced to His Son, Jesus Christ. After they have given their lives to Christ, the Lord gives you a lifetime to cultivate in them a hunger and a thirst for His Word and show them how to live in a way that honors and pleases Him. Simply, He's put your children in your life so you can be their primary discipler. With that said, you may have a number of questions. Probably your biggest question is 'how?' The answers to that question and many others are in the pages that follow...So let's begin the journey.

Hear, O Israel: The Lord our God, the Lord is one. Love the Lord your God with all your heart and with all your soul and with all your strength. These commandments that I give you today are to be on your hearts. Impress them on your children. Talk about them when you sit at home and when you walk along the road, when you lie down and when you get up. Tie them as symbols on your hands and bind them on your foreheads. Write them on the doorframes of your houses and on your gates. (Deut. 6:4-9)

"Here fix your center; here direct your aim; here concentrate your efforts, your energies, and your prayers. Remember, their religious education is your business. Whatever aids you call in from ministers or teachers, you never must, you never can, you never should, delegate this work. God will hold you responsible for the souls of your children."
— John Angell James

Day 1

Children are a heritage from the Lord, offspring a reward from Him. Like arrows in the hands of a warrior are children born in one's youth. Blessed is the man whose quiver is full of them. They will not be put to shame when they contend with their opponents in court. (Ps. 127:3-5)

Children's children are a crown to the aged, and parents are the pride of their children. (Prov. 17:6)

"The trouble with the rat race is that even if you win, you're still a rat."
— Jane Wagner

Ever walked out on your kids?

Not too many years ago I was standing outside the church's student center welcoming teenagers and their friends to our Wednesday night youth event. I always try to greet each teen as he or she comes into the building. One night two dads walked into the student center each with his teenager in tow. Without hesitation, I greeted the fathers and their children. We engaged in some small talk, and they went inside the building. It was refreshing to see these men leading their kids to church on a Wednesday night. I remember the thought running through my mind that these men were being great examples to their teens. Ten minutes later, as I was still welcoming arriving students, the same two dads walked past me on their way to the parking lot. This time they didn't stop to chat. As they walked past me I overheard one of them say, "We've got an hour; want to go get something to drink?" My earlier warm thoughts and feelings drained right out of me! I was speechless! As I watched them get into a car and pull out of the parking lot, several questions ran through my mind. "Why were these fathers dropping off their teens then leaving?" "Why were they not staying?" "We have adult programs running at the same time we have our youth event. Why didn't they go to one of those?" Needless to say, I felt reduced from being a youth pastor to a babysitter.

These two fathers showed me something that I had been missing for over twenty years of ministry. It occurred to me that there is a major misunderstanding in the minds of many parents. According to Deuteronomy 6, God explicitly gives parents the responsibility of teaching their children about Him and His Word. When God says in Deuteronomy 6:7a, "Impress them on your children" He's talking directly to the parents. Is this new news? In short, parents are commanded to be the primary disciplers of their children. Now I am realizing that more and more parents are disconnecting from their role as the primary discipler of their children and expecting someone else to spiritually educate them instead. In other words, parents are not taking the lead as disciplers. In essence, they are walking out on their responsibility!

A Look At The Current Situation

Why are so many parents walking away? Most couples, when given the privilege to become a parent, understand their role as primary provider and caregiver to their children. However, there is more to parenting than that. Not only are parents given the responsibility to take care of their children physically, but God also gives them the opportunity to be their spiritual caregiver as well. Unfortunately, a few too many parents tremble at the idea of playing the primary role of spiritual leader. Some would say that the church, the pastor, and the youth group are responsible for discipling, teaching, and training their children about God. Others would give the responsibility to Christian schools, civic organizations, coaches, family members, clubs or a combination of these to take the lead. While many of these groups and organizations can be a beneficial supplement in the course of a child's life, God considers these secondary to the parents.

Over the last several years, I have asked parents about their efforts in discipling their children and have received a number of different responses. One of the questions I have asked is, "Who is the primary discipler in your child's life?" Parents either do not know how to answer, change the subject, or begin to give me reasons why they are not doing a great job. I have found most parents actually know that discipleship is their responsibility. Nonetheless, parents are not comfortable with the task and try to explain away their rationale regarding their lack of participation in discipling their children. Here are a few of their answers:

- *"I have no influence on them! Other people have more impact than I do!"*
- *"I'm too busy; I don't have time!"*
- *"I have no idea how to disciple my kid, especially since I've never been discipled myself."*
- *"I'm raising my children alone. I have nobody else! It's only me."*
- *"I don't have a seminary degree. I can't possibly answer all their questions."*
- *"You're the paid professional; that's your job!"*
- *"My spouse is no help whatsoever. They show no interest nor see any need to disciple our children."*

Unfortunately, these were real statements made by parents when confronted with the idea of discipling their children. Parents are faced with the constant tension of the home, work, and community involvement. The demands of parenting are stressful, tiresome, and often a thankless responsibility. For some, time for family is a precious commodity. Parents are faced with the constant pressures of keeping employers satisfied, endless schedules of community activities, and relentless expectations of social trends. Many families have the added stress of one of the parents having little or no involvement when it comes to discipling their children. Unfortunately, blended and broken families also pose a great challenge in the disciple-making process. On top of that, many parents feel inadequate to disciple anyone due to the lack of their own spiritual development. As a result, parents find themselves frustrated and dependent on church staff or others to step in and become the disciplers of their own children. In other words, many families are not healthy because parents are not engaged in disciple-making!

Before you slam this book shut and throw it into the trashcan, relax and let me say one last thing. This book is only to encourage you. There will be some ideas and subjects in the next 24 days that will stretch and challenge you. However, I promise it is not my intention to drag you down or make you feel as if you don't measure up as a parent. Not by a long shot. This book is purposefully written to help you confront the issues of parental discipleship and use the Bible to train your kids in the way they should go. It doesn't matter if you're discipling your child as a single parent or a couple; this book will help you. So hang on tight, and let's get started.

God Has The Answer

What does God have to say about this situation? According to the Bible, God wants our families to be healthy. He has given His Word and the Holy Spirit to make health in the family a reality. God considers the parents the primary disciplers in the lives of their children. You are second to no one! God created the family to be the nucleus and incubator of a child's spiritual growth. Through the guidance of the Holy Spirit, God has given parents the responsibility for creating an environment suitable for their children to become followers of Christ.

In a passage found in Deuteronomy 6, Moses is delivering his farewell sermon to the children of Israel. His address is prior to the Israelites crossing the Jordan River and entering into the Promised Land. In this passage Moses is giving specific commands from God to ensure a long and prosperous life in the new land. Moses states:

> These are the commands, decrees and laws the Lord your God directed me to teach you to observe in the land that you are crossing the Jordan to possess, so that you, your children and their children after them may fear the Lord your God as long as you live by keeping all His decrees and commands that I give you, and so that you may enjoy long life. Hear, Israel, and be careful to obey so that it may go well with you and that you may increase greatly in a land flowing with milk and honey, just as the Lord, the God of your ancestors, promised you.
>
> Hear, O Israel: The Lord our God, the Lord is one. Love the Lord your God with all your heart and with all your soul and with all your strength. These commandments that I give you today are to be on your hearts. Impress them on your children. Talk about them when you sit at home and when you walk along the road, when you lie down and when you get up. Tie them as symbols on your hands and bind them on your foreheads. Write them on the doorframes of your houses and on your gates. (Deut. 6:1-9)

As you can see, God clearly gives the primary responsibility of discipling children to the parents. In verse seven God emphatically said, "Impress them on your children" (Deut. 6:7a). God was directing this statement straight to the father and mother. Notice how God clearly places the parents at the top of the discipleship process. The Lord has purposefully placed parents in this position because research has shown that they have the most influence in a child's life…more on that later.

Let me ask, how often do you have to repeat yourself to get your point across? In Deuteronomy 11 God does the same thing. In this passage, Moses reiterates these ideas of Deuteronomy 6 to emphasize the importance of his point. Moses says:

> Fix these words of mine in your hearts and minds; tie them as symbols on your hands and bind them on your foreheads. Teach them to your children, talking about them

when you sit at home and when you walk along the road, when you lie down and when you get up. Write them on the doorframes of your houses and on your gates, so that your days and the days of your children may be many in the land the Lord swore to give your ancestors, as many as the days that the heavens are above the earth. (Deut. 11:18-21)

Notice the Bible says, "Teach them to your children" (Deut. 11:19a). God uses Moses to underscore His desire for parents to take the lead in the discipleship development of each child in their home.

Perhaps disciple-making seems a bit overwhelming to you. You may not feel qualified for the responsibility. You may not know where you're going to find the time. Or you may be the only parent in your child's life. As a result, you're just not sure you should even try. Do not, I repeat, do not let any of these thoughts intimidate you. Instead, hold on to this one very important truth. God will never ask you to do anything that He will not amply and adequately supply you with all the needed resources to accomplish the task. Take, for example, Mary, the earthly mother of Jesus. At one point in her teenage life she found herself pregnant and on the brink of divorce. My guess is that Mary felt a bit overwhelmed during this time too. However, the Lord took care of every need and used her to bring Jesus to the planet and salvation to the world. Remember to hold onto the words Gabriel comforted Mary with after he announced she would give birth to the Son of God. The angel said, "Nothing, you see, is impossible with God" (Lk. 1:37 MSG).

Home Apps

Think back over the last few days of the last sermon, Bible study, Christian song, concert, etc…that you and your child heard together. Ask them questions about what they remember of the event. See if they can tell you anything about the Scriptures used, points made, illustrations given, or basic content during the experience. No need to grade them on this exercise; just observe how perceptive they were and how detailed their description is. The object of this test is to see how attentive they are to spiritual things and at what depth your child becomes engaged. If you implement this idea regularly, you and your child will be able to process Biblical truths in more detail and greatly improve your conversations.

Day 2

My people, hear my teaching; listen to the words of my mouth. I will open my mouth with a parable; I will utter hidden things, things from of old—things we have heard and known, things our ancestors have told us. We will not hide them from their descendants; we will tell the next generation the praiseworthy deeds of the Lord, His power, and the wonders He has done. He decreed statutes for Jacob and established the law in Israel, which He commanded our ancestors to teach their children, so the next generation would know them, even the children yet to be born, and they in turn would tell their children. Then they would put their trust in God and would not forget His deeds but would keep His commands. (Ps. 78:1-7)

"Pastor and theologian Jonathan Edwards had a far-reaching life and legacy. In 1900 A. E. Winship documented and listed only a few of the accomplishments associated with the 1,400 descendants of Edwards. He noted:

100 lawyers and a dean of a law school
80 holders of public office
66 physicians and a dean of a medical school
65 professors of colleges and universities
30 judges
13 college presidents
3 mayors of large cities
3 governors of states
3 United States senators
1 controller of the United States Treasury
1 Vice President of the United States

What kind of legacy will you and your mate leave? Will it be lasting? Will it be imperishable and eternal? Or will you leave behind only tangible items—buildings, money, and/or possessions?"
— Dennis and Barbara Rainey

Is the phrase, "like father, like son" really true?

Way, way back in 1967…I know you don't remember…television stations were required by law to run one anti-smoking commercial for every three cigarette commercials. One of the anti-smoking commercials begins with a father painting his home on top of a ladder that's leaning against his house. The camera slowly pans downward to show his young son painting away just like his dad on a much smaller ladder also leaning against the house. As the father and son team work on their project together, a voiceover announcer makes the statement, "Like father, like son." The next scene shows the father and son duo driving down the street in their Ford Mustang convertible, the dad behind the wheel and his son safely beside him in the customized car seat, complete with his own steering wheel. As they approach an intersection, the father puts his arm out of the window to signal to other drivers that he is about to make a left turn. Without hesitation, the son quickly copies his dad's hand signal and makes the same gesture outside his window. Next we see the father-son pair giving their Mustang a bath. In the background, the dad has a rag in one hand and a hosepipe in the other. The father is washing and rinsing the driver's side front fender. In the foreground the son is stooped low beside the passenger's side front tire. Just like dad, the son is working hard on the tire with his sponge for cleaning and a squirt gun for rinsing. As the men enjoy working together, the boy playfully pops up from his squatted position and surprises the dad by shooting him with his squirt gun. As the commercial continues, the father and son twosome are together taking a leisurely walk in their neighborhood. The dad sees a rock, bends down, picks up the rock, and tosses it into some woods. Just like his father, the son also finds a rock and throws it into the same patch of woods. The commercial's final scene has the tired father and son pair sitting next to a tree resting from their busy day of activities. The father reaches into his shirt pocket and pulls out a pack of cigarettes. He takes out a cigarette, lays down the pack beside his son, puts the cigarette to his lips, strikes a match, and lights it while his son quietly sits beside him observing his every move. As expected, the son looks down at the pack of cigarettes, picks it up, and curiously looks into the pack as if to mimic what he has just seen his father do. As the boy examines the cigarette pack, this time the voiceover announcer asks a question, "like father, like son? Think about it!"

Like it or not, believe it or not, this 1960's commercial is unbelievably accurate regarding the copycat nature of children. It is amazing how much influence parents have on their kids. This advertisement depicts the truth that children can and will imitate the things they see and hear, especially when displayed by their parents. Now my question is simply this: what do your kids see and hear from you that they imitate? It is probably more than you think.

Power of Influence Dilemma

Unfortunately, here's the problem. Many parents today think they have little or no real influence on their children. They believe that the truth of the 1960's commercial is not relevant or is outdated. When they are asked, parents say that friends, church leaders, teachers, media, and coaches have more input into the lives of children than they do. According to a variety of studies and surveys, parents are dead wrong. Parents, in all actuality, are by far the most influential people in a child's life. The idea that a child never wants the input of their parents is simply not true regardless of the child's age. How do I know this?

Wayne Rice and David Veerman state, "An extensive study of 272,400 teenagers conducted by USA Today Weekend Magazine found that 70 percent of teens identified their parents as the most important influences in their lives. Twenty-one percent said that about their friends (peers), and only 8 percent named the media."[1] It is staggering to see the gap between the parental influence percentage and the peer influence percentage. With a lead of forty-nine percentage points, the study indicates that parents are the most prominent people in a teenager's life. Ironically, a website of the Coors Brewing Company also adds, "Nearly three out of four parents believe their children's friends and classmates have the most influence… Yet contrary to what parents think, kids say Mom and Dad have the biggest impact on the choices they make."[2] This information is eye-opening. No wonder the brewing companies target adults so poignantly with their commercials and advertisements. They are extremely aware of the impact the father and mother have on their children. The media knows if they can entertain and entice adults with their advertising, their children are very likely to follow in their footsteps. Is the phrase "Like father, like son" ringing in your ears yet?

At this point you may feel there is a ray of hope with your younger children, but your older children are completely out of reach. You think that your influence with your teens is miniscule or non-existent. Let me say again, that too is dead wrong. In his book, *The Myth of Adolescence*, David Alan Black stated, "Secure relationships in the home are the primary source of significant adult relationships. Research reveals that the strongest influence on the life of a teenager is his or her parents. Parental influence decreases while peer influence increases each year through the ninth grade, but at no time does peer influence outweigh parental influence."[3]

It goes without saying that as you and your children grow older, your relationship changes. As the years pass, they mature and grow increasingly more independent. Don't be afraid of this transition. Make the necessary adjustments. Be willing to do whatever it takes to maintain a quality, secure relationship with them so you can continue to be a positive influence in their lives. As they face tough life issues and major decisions your wisdom will be invaluable. Please don't think I'm suggesting that you make compromises or support their craziness. That is not the case. However, the reality is that the days of diapers and sippy cups are a thing of the past and maintaining your influence is critical.

In Ephesians 6:4a the Bible says, "do not exasperate your children." "Exasperate" means to irritate intensely or infuriate. In this verse, "exasperate" is a pivotal word with a boatload of significance when dealing with older children. Since children are different, a wise parent needs to know how to relate to each of their children individually. Understand what pushes their buttons. Know when to speak and when to keep your mouth shut. In other words, pick your battles. Trying to fight every battle could easily "exasperate" them. Also, parents should never use their position to force their desires on their children. Just because you're the parent doesn't mean you should always get your way. That is not the goal. But possibly the biggest weapon unwise parents use that "exasperates" their children is guilt. Saying things like, "Why don't you call more often" or "You're always too busy for me" only produces a reaction based on frustration. When guilt is used, it has the potential to fracture or even sever the parent/child relationship.

Therefore, let me give a word of warning. As your children get older, failure to transition or adjust in your relationship could be risky. Your unwillingness to develop and maintain a quality relationship could result in your children gradually shutting you out of their lives. If this occurs, your influence really will be miniscule or non-existent.

What Matters Most

It is evident that children and teenagers take special notice of their parents' actions: good and bad. Parental influence is powerful! Studies have shown that Mom and Dad's influence reaches into many areas when it comes to the subject of religion. A study revealed by Ken Hemphill and Richard Ross in their book, *Parenting with Kingdom Purpose*, indicated, "The evidence clearly shows that the single most important social influence on the religious and spiritual lives of adolescents is their parents. Grandparents and other relatives, mentors, and youth workers can be very influential as well. But normally parents are most important in forming their children's religious and spiritual lives."[4] They go on to add, "Children and teenagers need parents and other adults in their lives who have a genuine, vibrant relationship with Jesus Christ."[5] Reggie Joiner and Carey Nieuwhof boldly say, "No one has more potential to influence your child than you… Your influence as a parent will be permanent."[6] Christian Smith, a leading researcher of youth culture, said in his book, *Soul Searching*, "Contrary to popular, misguided, cultural stereotypes and frequent parental misperceptions, we believe that the evidence clearly shows that the single most important social influence on the religious and spiritual lives of adolescents is their parents… This recognition may be empowering to parents, or alarming, or both."[7] Your influence is undeniable when it comes to your child's faith in Christ. The evidence is overwhelming! You have the ability to direct your children with incredible authority. Let me ask you a personal question. What are the kids in your life seeing and hearing from you, especially in your relationship with Jesus Christ?

Influence Now for the Future

I don't mean to be redundant, nor do I want to keep beating a dead horse; however, I need to go one more step. Do you realize that your baby, toddler, child, or teenager's spiritual future is potentially at risk here? The things they see and hear you do while they are growing up can and will affect their future spiritual beliefs. Bob Altemeyer, an associate professor in the Department of Psychology at the University of Manitoba, and Bruce Hunsberger, a professor of psychology at Wilfred Laurier University, retold the stories of forty-six college freshmen in their book, *Amazing Conversations*. These college freshmen state, "We acquire our religion from our parents almost as certain as we inherit the color of our eyes."[8] Altemeyer and Hunsberger go on to add, "You can make a pretty good prediction of whether or not a university student, raised as a Christian, will still accept Christianity if you know how much the family religion was emphasized while he was growing up."[9] Startling, isn't it?

Therefore, let me ask you a few personal questions about the children who will eventually leave your home and start lives of their own. Do you want them to have:

- *A salvation that is based on faith in Jesus Christ – Ephesians 2:8-9?*
- *A real love relationship with the Father – Psalms 27:4?*
- *A display of the fruit of the Holy Spirit in their lives – Galatians 5:22-23?*
- *A genuine devotion to their families, especially their spouses – Ephesians 5:22, 25?*
- *A heart to invest their time and money to the local church – Hebrews 10:25?*
- *A vision to see the lost come to Christ – Matthew 28:19-20 & Acts 1:8?*

Then guess who's going to be the primary one to show these truths to your child? You guessed it: Tag! You're it! Your kids need you, and rest assured, God will supply.

There is little doubt that God has given this ominous task of discipling the child to you without reservation, and for good reason. You are the most influential person in your children's lives, especially in matters of faith. There is no one who comes close to being more qualified for the job than you. Alan Melton and Paul Dean said, "There are many reasons that no one can disciple your child better than you. First of all, there is no one who has the availability to disciple your children like you... No one else loves your children like you do... No one naturally knows your children better than you and your spouse... No one else is commanded by the Lord to disciple your children."[10] According to all indications, you have the most influence, the greatest interest, and are held most accountable; therefore, there is no one better suited for the job than you. Are you up for the challenge?

Home Apps

As you go through the next few days, secretly observe some specific things about your children. Watch them as they play and interact with others. Pay close attention to their mannerisms, how they stand, and how they walk. Listen to the words they use. Study how they use phrases and pronounce words. After you've had a chance to take a few notes, look at your findings and consider this question. What characteristics do you see in each of your children that are most like you? Next, take the same list and see if there are any resemblances to their other parent. These similarities are not coincidental when you consider the power of your influence.

Day 3

Fix these words of mine in your hearts and minds; tie them as symbols on your hands and bind them on your foreheads. Teach them to your children, talking about them when you sit at home and when you walk along the road, when you lie down and when you get up. Write them on the doorframes of your houses and on your gates, so that your days and the days of your children may be many in the land the Lord swore to give your ancestors, as many as the days that the heavens are above the earth. If you carefully observe all these commands I am giving you to follow—to love the Lord your God, to walk in obedience to Him and to hold fast to Him. (Deut. 11:18-22)

"Don't say you don't have enough time. You have exactly the same number of hours per day that were given to Helen Keller, Pasteur, Michaelangelo, Mother Teresa, Leonardo da Vinci, Thomas Jefferson, and Albert Einstein."
— H. Jackson Brown

"Day, n. A period of twenty-four hours, mostly misspent."
— Ambrose Bierce

"A person's days are determined; You have decreed the number of his months and have set limits he cannot exceed."
— Job

Is time really on your side?

USA Today did an investigation concerning how people use their time. The newspaper commissioned a team of researchers to discover what the average person says he or she wants to do on any given day. The group determined a typical person wants to have time for sleeping, eating, doing housework, spiritual edification, working their job, commuting, hygiene, entertainment, and exercise. As a result, the group determined the average person needs 42 hours per day just to do what he or she wants to do. You know as well as I do that we are each given only 24 hours per day: that translates into 1,440 minutes per day, which comes outs to 86,400 seconds per day. No matter how you slice it, there is never enough time; nor will there ever be enough time to do what we want to do. On the other hand, there is always enough time to do the things we need to do. How do I know this? Let's take a look at the life of Jesus.

Jesus was given just three short years to change the world. God sent His Son to earth to choose and train twelve men, redirect the religious thinking from law to grace, display to the world through His teaching and healing ministry that He is actually the Son of God, go to the cross, die, go to the grave, come back from the grave, and return to heaven. Jesus may not have had enough time to do all the things He wanted to do. However, Jesus had more than enough time to do what He needed to do. That's why Jesus said to the Father just before He went to the cross, "I have brought you glory on earth by finishing the work you gave me to do" (Jn. 17:4).

Just like Jesus, we may not be able to accomplish the things we want to do before we die. It's very likely there will be a few items left on our "bucket list" when we pass away from this world. However, just as He did for Jesus, God will give us more than enough time to do the things He needs us to do. With that said, as a parent, let me ask you a question. What do you think God needs you to do? In other words, what is the primary mission He has given you to accomplish as a parent? The answer is simple…disciple your children.

God's Primary Mission to Parents

I know as parents you are busy people. You have to juggle work, home, church, school events, social activities, and family just to name a few. As a result, time becomes a precious commodity. With all the responsibilities, commitments, and demands of life, discipling your kids can be an incredible challenge. I have great news! God's Word is full of guidance and direction. Scripture shows parents how they can naturally make disciples of their children. Within the Old Testament books of Deuteronomy and Proverbs, the Bible gives parents everything they need to know regarding how to honor God as a discipler. Let's take a look.

In the book of Deuteronomy, Moses delivered his farewell sermon to the children of Israel. Just prior to the Israelites crossing the Jordan River and entering into the Promised Land, Moses gave specific commands from God to ensure a long and prosperous life in the new land. Moses stated,

Hear, O Israel: The Lord our God, the Lord is one. Love the Lord your God with all your heart and with all your soul and with all your strength. These commandments that I give you today are to be on your hearts. Impress them on your children. Talk about them when you sit at home and when you walk along the road, when you lie down and when you get up. Tie them as symbols on your hands and bind them on your foreheads. Write them on the doorframes of your houses and on your gates. (Deut. 6:4-9)

God, through Moses, clearly gives the primary responsibility of discipleship to the parents of their sons and daughters. God did so because He knew the dangers that awaited the Israelites just on the other side of the river. The Canaanite people worshipped idols. One idol named Molek was the god of purity. The Canaanites believed that to satisfy Molek they were required to sacrifice their children to him. According to Proverbs 6:17b, the Lord hates "hands that shed innocent blood." There were grave consequences associated with falling into idol worship. The Bible says, "Any Israelite or any foreigner residing in Israel who sacrifices any of his children to Molek is to be put to death. The members of the community are to stone him" (Lev. 20:2). Obviously God is serious about His commands.

Therefore, in Moses' sermon, the Lord revealed His design for the family. First, the phrase "Love the Lord your God with all heart and with all your soul and with all your strength" (Deut. 6:5) has a specific point. God wanted all His people to love Him with all their being and hold nothing back. God demanded that He be the only, one, true God in their lives. Secondly, the phrase "are to be upon your hearts" (Deut. 6:6b) has a direct purpose. God wanted the following commands to be rooted and secured in their hearts first. His commands were not for casual thought. On the contrary, God desired His Word to be first and foremost in their thinking, attitudes, speech, and actions. Thirdly, the phrase "impress them on your children" (Deut. 6:7a) has several implications. The Lord directed His commands to the parents of the 'children.' In other words, God directed this statement straight at you and me. God clearly implied that parents are at the top of the discipleship process. God commanded the parents to love Him with all their being and transfer that love to their children. God's instructions were simple and specific. He directed them to talk about His commands when they sit together, walk together, go to bed, and get up in the morning. In other words, while parents spend time with their children, they should intentionally make God a natural part of their conversation. God is not suggesting that parents are to force a spiritual conversation. Actually, God expects parents to love Him so much that their love for Him becomes a normal expression of their lives. Believers are to be so focused and filled with love for the Lord that it overflows in every aspect of their lives. To genuinely love the Lord with all their hearts, souls, and strength would require parents to have a philosophy similar to that of Joshua 1:8 (J1.8). Joshua stated, "Do not let this Book of the Law depart from your mouth; meditate on it day and night, so that you may be careful to do everything written in it. Then you will be prosperous and successful" (Josh. 1:8). When parents practice loving the Lord with all their hearts, souls, and strength, they constantly talk about God, think about God, and carefully obey God. Does this describe you? If not, it can. With God, it is never too late. If it does describe you, are you ready to go deeper?

Let me ask again: how often do you have to repeat yourself to get your point across to your kids? Just consider it a Godly characteristic. As mentioned in the reading of Day 1, it is not a coincidence that Moses repeated almost the same words and phrases later in his sermon to the Israelites only five short chapters later. In Deuteronomy 11, the Lord knew that the people would need to hear His commands a second time to let them know the importance of His desires. So, what is the point? We have to see the importance of God's command. It is critical that we love God with every fiber of our being and allow Him to consume every aspect of our lives.

The Bible doesn't stop there. This same sentiment is also implied in the book of Proverbs. In chapter 22, Solomon gave explicit instruction to parents in one short verse when he said, "Train up a child in the way he should go: and when he is old, he will not depart from it" (Prov. 22:6 KJV). Solomon, known as the wisest man to ever live, was giving godly advice to parents from the standpoint of being a parent.

In his book, *Hopeful Parenting: Encouragement for Raising Kids Who Love God*, David Jeremiah asked the question, "What does it mean to 'train up'"?[11] He gave a compelling answer to that question:

> *The term is used in the Old Testament just three other times, in all three instances to convey the idea of dedication: once to describe the dedication of Solomon's house, twice to convey the idea of dedicating the temple. The word originally related to the palate of the mouth. An Arab midwife would rub crushed dates on the palate of a baby's mouth to stimulate the instinctive action to suck, so that the child could be nourished. Over time the concept of training up came to mean "to create a thirst or a hunger within a child for the godly things of life." Sometimes we've given the concept a military flavor. "Get in shape!" "I'm training you up, boy!" But it's not like that at all. This isn't boot camp; it has to do with creating within the child a thirst and a hunger for the things of God.[12]*

The word "train" obviously has the idea of intentionality and determination. God holds the parents responsible for producing in their children's lives a hungering and thirsting after the Lord. In other words, parents should reproduce an improved copy of themselves. At the end of verse 6, God gives parents a glimpse into each child's future when He says, "When he is old, he will not depart from it" (Prov. 22:6b KJV). Even though there are no guarantees, these words help motivate, give hope, and provide encouragement to parents in the good and difficult times of child rearing. In his book *Already Gone*, Ken Ham adds this commentary regarding Proverbs 22:6: "What a reminder to teach children from when they are born – and a reminder to be diligent in providing the right sort of training/curricula, etc., for children."[13]

How to Accomplish the Mission

Last Christmas a friend of mine bought each of her sons the latest iPod touch. That was not really a big deal except that her boys were nine and ten years old. Maybe I'm old-fashioned, but I was a little surprised that she was giving her young sons these gifts. I was not surprised because they were expensive, high tech toys but because these small devices have tremendous ability to access X-rated materials if not properly supervised.

On Christmas day her two boys were very excited to get their iPods. I showed them some basic features of how to work them, and they were captivated. Later that day I asked the mom how she was planning on monitoring what her boys downloaded on their iPods from the iTunes store. I could tell I must have slipped into speaking another language because she was clueless. The mom was a little puzzled and asked me what I was talking about. I picked up one of the iPods and showed the mom just how easy it was to pull up to view and potentially download what is considered "adult material" on this small device. Then, to my surprise, the mom looked at me and said, "I don't have time to keep up with that!"

With today's hectic pace of life, parents sometimes have a hard time distinguishing between what they want to do and what they need to do. How do busy parents in today's society accomplish the Biblical mandate of discipling their children? There is one key ingredient you need to consider. If you will dare to implement this crucial element, you may discover you have more time to do the things God needs you to do as a parent. You have to restructure your vocabulary.

The suggestion may require a great deal of effort. Vocabulary restructuring is difficult to do when you're out of practice. Parents need the time to be intentional about discipleship. To make this happen requires the implementation of a one-syllable, two-letter declaration into their language arsenal. The word is No! Learn to say it. This may take some reprogramming on your part, but it can be done. Saying no is very difficult for many people, but it will provide you with much-needed time for investing in your kids. You need to be selective with their time outside the home in order to protect the time necessary for the family to naturally come together. In other words, you need to say no to busyness in order to streamline the time they have as a family. This does not mean you have to say no to everything; that's not what is meant at all. However, you do need to say no to whatever gets in the way of your being obedient to the Lord. It could mean saying no to some of the "wants" in your life in order to have time for the "needs." It could mean saying no to some of your children's "wants" in order to free up the time for their greater "need."

In his book, *Margin*, Richard Swenson gave this illustration. He said, "When Steve Jobs took over Apple Computer for the second time in 1998, he preached that the company needed a prioritizing plan to rediscover its main emphasis. 'Focus does not mean saying yes,' explained Jobs, 'it means saying no.' His words speak to many of our lives as well."[14] When parents learn to strategically say no, they will be able to talk about God more, think about God more, and obey God more fully. This is the first crucial step in freeing up the much-needed time you've been missing.

God's requirements are simple; however, some restructuring may be required. Again, implementing no into your vocabulary doesn't mean saying no to everything. However, it does mean saying no to whatever gets in the way of fulfilling your responsibility. One word of caution: you should make these changes slowly. Don't freak your family out by saying no to everything and making wholesale schedule changes. This will cause unnecessary frustration. However, discuss the necessary changes with your family and tell them why you are making the needed changes. If you will do what God asks, the Lord can do miracles.

Home Apps

Are you someone who constantly runs in a million different directions? Do you find it hard to use that pesky little two-letter word no? Have you been struggling with how to accomplish God's mission for your children? Then this exercise could be beneficial. Make a list of all the activities you're involved in outside of your home. Everything goes on the list except your job and regular church events. Basically, what are you doing when you are not at home, work, or church? Perhaps nothing on your list is wrong in and of itself, but juggling numerous obligations at the same time can cause weariness. Now that you have your list, ask yourself this question in light of the assignment God has given you: What is getting in the way of discipling my children better? In other words, what do I need to say no to in order to free up some much needed time so I can improve my disciple-making in my family?

Day 4

It's better to have a partner than go it alone. Share the work, share the wealth. And if one falls down, the other helps, but if there's no one to help, tough! Two in a bed warm each other. Alone, you shiver all night. By yourself you're unprotected. With a friend you can face the worst. (Ecc. 4:9-12a MSG)

"I challenge you to think of one act of genuine significance in the history of humankind that was performed by a lone human being (apart from the redemptive work of Christ on the cross). No matter what you name, you will find that a team of people was involved."
— John C. Maxwell

Need help?

Derek Redmond was born to run. Redmond, born in Bletchley, Buckinghamshire, England, held the British record for the 400-meter sprint. He also won several gold medals in the 4x400 meter relay at the Commonwealth Games, European Championships, and World Championships. However, Redmond is best remembered for his performance at the 1992 Olympic Games in Barcelona. As a favorite to win Olympic Gold, Derek entered the semi-final race poised in lane five. Derek started the race well. Unfortunately, in the final leg of the sprint, his hamstring snapped. He hobbled to an abrupt stop then fell to the track in severe pain, holding his right thigh. As the medics rushed to assist him, Derek waved them off because his goal was to finish the race. He slowly stood and began to hobble down the track. As he made his way down the last 200 meters, his father Jim Redmond broke through security and joined his son on the track. Distraught but determined, Derek leaned on his dad's shoulder and limped across the finish line dead last. As they crossed the finish, the crowd of 65,000 gave Derek and his father a standing ovation. Redmond, according to Olympic officials, was disqualified from the race. Today, the Olympic records state that Derek Redmond "did not finish" the race. However, that's not entirely true. He and his father did finish the race. Both finished the race together!

There is never a case, never an instance, and never a situation that we don't need help. Sometimes a little help is needed; sometimes a great deal of help is needed. No matter what the circumstance, we need each other. This is especially true when it comes to discipleship.

Church Mandate

The New Testament talks a lot about the importance of parents' discipling their children. The Apostle Paul gave explicit instruction to the church regarding discipleship in the home. Even though Paul never married nor had any children, he was inspired by the Holy Spirit to give instruction in this area. Paul said in Ephesians 6:4, "Fathers, do not exasperate your children; instead, bring them up in the training and instruction of the Lord." Before parents can accomplish the task of "training and instruction," they need to be trained and instructed themselves. The question has to be asked, "Where do parents get this training and instruction?" The answer lies in the church. God desires both the parents and the church to come alongside each other to work together as a team to make sure they cross the finish line together. The two need each other!

Why does the answer lie in the church? According to Ephesians 4:11-12 the Bible says, "So Christ Himself gave…pastors and teachers, to equip His people for works of service, so that the body of Christ may be built up." In other words, Christ has provided spiritually mature people in the church to give Biblical training and instruction to equip parents as disciple-makers. Because the Lord has charged the church with a great responsibility, it has a major task to accomplish. God has high standards and expectations for pastors and their staff. It is their job to train moms and dads so they can do the discipling they are called to do. Barna stated, "Parents are not so much unwilling to provide more substantive training to their children as they are ill-equipped to do such work."[15]

If Barna's statement is true, then the church has a very important and critical job. It is the duty of the church to provide Biblical teaching in relevant and practical ways so that parents are able to know and understand God's Word on every subject pertaining to life. Another way of putting it is, "The church must train parents how to train."[16] This is very important, especially for parents who have never been discipled themselves. I know for some this may seem overwhelming. Don't let it. Everyone needs spiritually mature believers in their lives. That's why the Bible says, "As iron sharpens iron, so one person sharpens another" (Prov. 27:17). Do you have someone mentoring or discipling you? Remember: the best place to get that assistance is in the church. That means that the church and the home must work together as a team.

Church and Home Working as a Team

Are you working together as a team?

Two old farmers entered their horses in a horse pull competition. The object of the contest was to hitch the animal to a weighted sled and have the horse attempt to pull the sled a certain distance. The first farmer's horse won first place by pulling a 700-pound sled. The other farmer's horse finished second. The runner-up horse was only able to pull a 500-pound sled. After the contest the two farmers decided to hitch both horses together to see just how much weight they could pull together. Many people assumed that the two animals would pull 1,200 pounds. To everyone's amazement both horses together pulled the 1,200-pound sled with ease. They didn't stop there. The horses pulled 1,400, 1,600, even an 1,800-pound sled. The farmers kept adding weight to the sled and the two horses together were able to astonish the crowd by pulling 1,900 pounds. This is an awesome illustration of the importance of teamwork. God has designed the church and the home to come together as a team when it comes to discipleship. The church is commanded to provide the equipping, and the parents are commanded to be the primary disciplers of their children. When the two come together, God can do some incredible things in the life of the family.

Now the question is, "Where do we start?" Today, there are more resources and programs focused on teaching God's inherent truth than ever before. Churches have access to an enormous amount of Bible study materials from well-known and qualified theologians. Pastors have the ability to find an almost unlimited supply of curriculum designed specifically to lead people to a deeper walk in their journey with the Lord. The church, now more than ever, is very well-equipped with the resources they need to make disciples. Steve Wright stated, "The church must excel in instructing and equipping moms and dads in all aspects of family life, especially discipling their children."[17] Therefore, the church has the responsibility to provide discipleship opportunities for the entire family with excellence. When the church strives to do this, they are fulfilling God's command, "Go and make disciples" (Matt. 28:19a).

I will be the first to say that pastors and staff are commanded by the Lord to offer discipleship opportunities with quality and excellence. It is time for pastors to roll up their sleeves and get to work equipping "people for works of service, so that the body of Christ may be built up" (Eph. 4:12).

Discipleship will cost pastors and staff everything they've got, but it will be the greatest investment of their ministry. So pastors, let's get to work!

However, the door swings both ways. You and your family need to take advantage of the church's discipleship offerings and get fully engaged. Parents should strategically and purposefully integrate their family into a local church that stands on solid Biblical teaching and offers quality discipleship opportunities.

How connected are you with what your church offers regarding discipleship? Parents today have the chance to engage in small groups, discipleship groups, mentoring, and prayer groups to become growing disciples. However, there is a sad reality. Many parents have used the church not so much for their own spiritual edification but as a place to drop off their kids so the paid professionals can provide Biblical education for their children. Many parents are not engaging, and this lack of teamwork has to end. The church and the home need to come together, work together, and even pull together as one. When both institutions are unified, they will take each other across the finish line together.

The Bottom Line

Training and discipling aspects for parents can come in a variety of ways within the church that will pay big dividends. It is the responsibility of parents to take advantage of as many of those opportunities as possible. The Lord is able to use sermons, small groups, personal discipleship ministries, and many other resources to help parents develop a growing knowledge of Scripture. The bottom line is that it's up to you to make it happen. As your knowledge increases, you will not be intimidated by hard theological questions from your children. As you grow, you will be able to search Scripture and answer even the most difficult questions they present. Even if you are not able to discover the answers to difficult questions, you'll be able to utilize other people in the church to help answer the hardest questions. God has established the church and given the home to you. According to Steve Wright, "The home is responsible for training children, but the church is responsible for equipping parents in how to train their children."[18] The church and the home have the potential to be the most viable and influential institutions for discipling kids when both work together as a team. Are you determined to invest the time to become a genuine disciple of Christ? A seminary or Bible college degree is not required. Using the church to become the disciplers your children need is actually God's design. Then you will be able to provide the needed guidance for your children to become the disciples God desires them to be. George Barna states, "Revolutionary parents see their church as an invaluable partner in a long-term effort to raise a mature follower of Christ."[19]

Home Apps

How well do you know your church staff? Take time to get acquainted with the paid and volunteer staff at your church. In particular, get to know the men and women that have responsibility in the areas in which your children participate. Invite them over to your home for coffee or a meal. Be determined to get to know them on a personal level. Understand their ministry philosophy, vision, and goals in their areas of responsibility. In other words, find out the direction of their ministry and what your children are experiencing. Once you've had a chance to meet them, ask yourself a few questions: How well do their plans matchup with what the Lord has given me to do? Will the direction of their ministries supplement my disciple-making efforts? Do our endeavors complement one another? These are important questions to consider as you move forward together.

Day 5

Can you round up a third? A three-stranded rope isn't easily snapped. (Ecc. 4:12b)

Because we loved you so much, we were delighted to share with you not only the gospel of God but our lives as well. (1 Thess. 2:8)

Mentor, n. "A man who fundamentally affects and influences the development of another man."
— Dr. Bill Bennett

Who's on your team?

Early one Friday morning I was sitting in the Wilmington, North Carolina iHop with Dr. Bill Bennett, my mentor. Dr. Bennett, a very godly man, has been my mentor for over thirteen years. But because of traveling distance and mostly busyness on my part, it had been about three years since we had seen each other face to face. During that three-year period, we talked on the phone occasionally, but I had not made the time nor given the effort to stay connected. The Lord started convicting me about my neglect. God had placed Dr. Bennett in my life for a reason, and I was not utilizing him the way I should. While we were waiting for our breakfast order, he asked me what I wanted from him. I knew I needed to reconnect with him, but I wasn't sure what to say. It had been three years and I was the reason for the lack of communication. It was a humiliating and awkward moment, but I knew I was being disobedient to the Lord by not allowing God to use him in my life. I asked Dr. Bennett if he would forgive me and come back into my life to help challenge me, encourage me, and disciple me. He looked me straight in the eye and without hesitation said, "Yes, of course I will." He handed me his card and said, "I want you to call me anytime. Day or night you can call on me!" By that time our waitress arrived with our order, and the rest of our time was as if we had never been apart.

The reason I mention this story is simple. We all need someone in our lives to help us grow. I need someone and so do you. The Christian life cannot be lived in a vacuum. In other words, we can't go through life all alone. We need people who will ask us the hard questions about our lives. It is important that we allow family and friends to confront us with our thoughts, attitudes, speech, and actions. God gives us one another so that together we can grow in the likeness of Christ. Take the Apostle Paul for instance. At one point in his life he hated and even killed Christians. But he had an encounter with Jesus on the Damascus Road and became one of the most tenacious theologians and preachers of the gospel. He is also responsible for writing thirteen books of the New Testament. Quite impressive. Did he do it alone in a vacuum? Not at all! The Lord sent a man named Barnabas into his life to mentor him. See my point? Therefore, it is of utmost importance that we have other significant people to share their lives to help us grow.

Significant Others

Without a doubt, the Lord has given parents the ominous task of discipling their kids. On top of that, God expects the church to come alongside the parents to give them the needed assistance and support in the discipleship process. Even though the Bible is clear about the job of the parent and the church, God does not expect us to do it alone. The Lord has given other important components for parents to utilize. In the Deuteronomy 6 passage there is a phrase that often is unnoticed. In verse four the Bible says in Deuteronomy 6:4a, "Hear, O Israel." To the casual reader this would seem to be just an introduction with little to no significance, but this is not the case. Moses is actually calling the whole congregation of Israel to attention and accountability to what he's about to say. The commands outlined in verses 4b – 9 are given specifically to the parents. However, the Lord is also strategically commanding the entire nation to take part in the discipleship process. Not only was Moses speaking to the parents during his message, but he was also addressing grandparents, aunts, uncles, and the extended community as well.

> *The Hebrew culture described in Deuteronomy naturally promoted this kind of relationship. We're challenged to rethink our understanding of family, as the Fuller Youth Institute explains: "A family in the Old Testament would have included parents, children, workers, perhaps adult siblings with their own spouses and children. In fact, households could be compiled of as many as eighty people. These texts, such as Deuteronomy 6, are discussing the communal raising of children. Our own cultural distance from these passages may cause us to put undue pressure on parents alone."[20]*

Even though we live in a different time and culture, there is much to learn from the Hebrew people. Today families do not typically have eighty family members living nearby, much less in the same house. However, we can purposefully recruit godly family members who also have a vested interest in our children's lives to help disciple them. It is critical for parents to enlist people they know and trust to come alongside them to assist in the daunting task of discipling their children.

Parents need all the help they can get when it comes to the discipleship process. Verse four also indicates another valuable resource at the parent's disposal. Parents should utilize godly people from the church and community to assist in their discipleship efforts. These people are not to take the place of the parents but to supplement the work of the parents. Reggie Joiner said, "The goal is for you to pursue strategic relationships so another adult voice will be speaking into your son's or daughter's life, saying the kinds of things you would try to say as a parent."[21] No matter if you're a single parent disciple-maker, the only parent in the home motivated to discipling, or a couple working together as disciplers, your task is the same. Make sure you are strategically placing godly people in the lives of your children. This responsibility can be very difficult and trying. Obviously this duty should not be taken lightly. Parents should seek the Lord in this effort. James 1:5 says, "If any of you lacks wisdom, you should ask God, who gives generously to all without finding fault, and it will be given to you." In short the Bible is saying, "ask God to give you wisdom." Let me ask…who loves you the most? Answer: God does! Who loves your children the most? Answer again: God does! Who wants the very best for you and your children? Of course, God does! Oh, and by the way, God also loves your children more than you do, so we can trust Him with His plan. Therefore asking God to give you wisdom to utilize family and friends in the discipleship process is of utmost importance.

Advantage of the Investment

In an article published by Lifeway, Mark Kelly indicated the importance of having another adult intentionally spend time with a teenager. Time spent today is actually an investment in the kid's future. Kelly said, "Teens who had at least one adult from church make a significant time investment in their lives also were more likely to keep attending church. More of those who stayed in church – by a margin of 46 percent to 28 percent – said five or more adults at church had invested time with them personally and spiritually."[22] Based on this research, parents could potentially affect the adult lives of their teens in a positive way. Proactive parents who take the time to allow positive adult influences can help their children become faithful church attendees later in life. He went on to say, "Investing time in young people lives out the love of Jesus Christ in a tangible way. It proves that a young person belongs at church. It can help connect the dots to help a teen integrate their faith into their life. And it gives the teen a connection to church after graduation when many of their peers are no longer around."[23] It is vital for a parent to purposefully seek out other godly people who will add value to their discipleship efforts.

You may be thinking, "Is this really worth it?" "Do I have the time?" "Do I need to go to all the trouble of looking for and, to a point, interviewing someone to supplement my discipleship efforts?" Let me share an e-mail I received from John Richardson not long ago. He was a former student of mine when I was a part-time youth pastor in High Point, North Carolina. Read what he wrote and I'll let you decide for yourself.

> *Hey Mark,*
>
> *It has been a long time since we've seen or talked with each other. I just wanted to write and share with you what God has been doing in my life. I also hope this encourages you to continue in the ministry. Recently, I left North Carolina and moved to Chattanooga, Tennessee to follow God's will. The Lord has called me into full time ministry. I am now the campus pastor at Tennessee Temple University. I wanted to thank you for investing in me when I was a teenager and making a difference in my life. God has used you to build a foundation in my life that is now influencing others. I have not forgotten all the times you came to my house and picked up my brother and me for church. I have also not forgotten the mission trips the youth group went on. I can still remember all the work you and your family put into making the mission trips happen even while you worked a full time secular job and only worked at the church part-time. I was blessed by your willingness to serve. I pray that I can minister to students as you've done for me and countless others. I hope this encourages you and allows you to understand the value of your life in God's plan. Thank you so much.*
>
> *Keep your hand to the plow,*
> *John*

Do not underestimate the impact of strategically having a godly person in your child's life…no matter if the person is a relative or a friend of the family. I cannot stress this point enough.

Let me give you a list of items to consider when praying and pursuing someone to come alongside you in the discipleship efforts of your children. You need to see evidence of these:

- *Salvation based on faith in Jesus Christ – Ephesians 2:8-9.*
- *A real love relationship with the Father – Psalms 27:4.*
- *The fruit of the Holy Spirit in their lives – Galatians 5:22-23.*
- *Real devotion to their family, especially their spouse – Ephesians 5:22, 25.*
- *Investment of their time and money to the local church – Hebrews 10:25.*
- *Vision to see the lost come to Christ – Matthew 28:19-20 and Acts 1:8.*

To answer the questions: "Is it worth it? Do I have the time? Do I need to go to all the trouble of looking for and interviewing someone to supplement my discipleship efforts?" The answer is: "Absolutely!" Your kid's future spiritual health is riding on the decisions you make today. Don't waste your chance.

Home Apps

Finding significant others to supplement your discipleship efforts can be a great experience. At dinner tonight or while you're driving down the road, ask your children who the other adults are in their lives. Find out who they look up to. Don't hesitate to add a few names after they've named some people. These could be teachers, neighbors, coaches, small group leaders, pastors, and relatives. Who among the list are people you trust? Do they have a growing relationship with the Lord? Do they embrace the same Biblical values you hold? Take the next several weeks and ask God for wisdom. During this time pay close attention to the people God reveals to you. Are they people that can come alongside and help you disciple your child? This could be the start of a life-long mentoring relationship.

IT ALL STARTS WITH YOU

Read This First – Week 2 Intro...

Every fire starts with a spark. When it comes to discipleship, parents are the sparks that ignite the family. Now that you are an expert on the Deuteronomy 6 and Proverbs 22:6 passages, you are more than qualified to be that igniter. But before you start any fires, use the next 5 days of reading to get the gas cans filled and your wood ready.

In Days 6 through 10, your reading will be about you. We will shift our discussion from developing a strategy for discipleship to developing as a discipler. That's why this week is entitled "It All Starts with You." It's about your relationship with Christ and how to make God's Word real in your life. However, there is one word of caution. Since this week's reading is all about you, don't be surprised if God begins to ignite a fire in you. Before the week is out, you may be repeating the same words the two fellows walking to Emmaus stated. The two men said, "Were not our hearts burning within us while He talked with us on the road and opened the Scriptures to us" (Lk. 24:32)?

And be thankful. Let the message of Christ dwell among you richly as you teach and admonish one another with all wisdom through psalms, hymns, and songs from the Spirit, singing to God with gratitude in your hearts. And whatever you do, whether in word or deed, do it all in the name of the Lord Jesus, giving thanks to God the Father through Him. (Col. 3:15b-17)

"No matter what you teach the child, he insists on behaving like his parents."
— James Merritt

"Each day of our lives we make deposits in the memory banks of our children."
— Charles R. Swindoll

Day 6

Make every effort to live in peace with everyone and to be holy; without holiness no one will see the Lord. (Heb. 12:14)

As obedient children, do not conform to the evil desires you had when you lived in ignorance. But just as He who called you is holy, so be holy in all you do; for it is written: "Be holy, because I am holy." (1 Pet. 1:14-16)

"Many times when we are discouraged, we think, I don't want to be around Christians. I don't want to read the Bible. I don't want to pray. But that is a big mistake. That is when we ought to be running to God, not away from Him. We ought to be spending time with His people and in His Word, not avoiding them."
— Greg Laurie

Are your kids being held back?

Do you consider yourself to be a good parent or a great parent? If you see yourself as a good parent, would you like to bump up to great? If you see yourself as a great parent, would you like to be an awesome parent? You can! You can even do it without making your life more cluttered and complicated.

Recapping last week, we see God makes it clear that He holds parents responsible to be the primary disciplers in their children's lives. Based on Deuteronomy 6:4-9 and Proverbs 22:6, God unmistakably gives parents full responsibility to make disciples of their children. Parents are also instructed to utilize the church and strategically enlist others in the disciple-making process. Sounds good on paper, but how can parents who are already overloaded make this work?

Many parents feel they are too busy, not qualified, or just not cool enough to have influence in their kid's lives to make discipleship work for them. To that I say, "If you're too busy, maybe you need to jettison some things on your schedule." Yes you are qualified! As a matter of fact you are more than qualified. Okay, even though you may not be that cool, you actually have the greatest influence in your child's life. This is God-given. Not only that, it is God designed. How do I know this? Allow me to reiterate a main point from chapter one. Secular surveys and studies have been conducted that consistently prove that parents are the most influential people in their children's lives. The MTV network did a nationwide study and discovered how influential parents are to their viewers. They asked their audience between the ages of 13 and 24 the question, "What makes you happy?"[1] The study revealed this observation:

> A worried, weary parent might imagine the answer to sound something like this: Sex, drugs, a little rock 'n' roll. Maybe some cash, or at least the car keys. Turns out the real answer is quite different. Spending time with family was the top answer to that open-ended question… Parents are seen as an overwhelmingly positive influence in the lives of most young people. Remarkably, nearly half of teens mention at least one of their parents as a hero.[2]

Simply put, kids like their parents. God designed this honor for parents and desires for parents to obey His command to influence their children by discipling them.

However, before parents can disciple their children, there are some conditions that must be considered. To be an effective disciple-maker of your children, God expects you to be pursuing a strong and vibrant relationship with Him first. John Maxwell once said, "People cannot give to others what they themselves do not possess."[3] Before you can disciple anyone, you need to be growing spiritually. Spiritual growth takes determination and dedication. In her book *Spiritual Parenting*, Michelle Anthony discussed the importance of disciplers taking responsibility for their own spiritual development:

Before I can be responsible for anyone else, I must take responsibility for me. This is not a selfish act, but a necessary one. My friend Roger Tirabassi illustrated this point well when he said that the airline companies understand this concept when they instruct passengers, "In the event of an emergency, if you are traveling with a child, first put on your own oxygen mask before putting on the mask of your child." By taking responsibility for myself, I am in a better position to offer myself to others.[4]

It is bizarre to think that anyone can possibly help another person develop as a disciple of Christ when there is no personal commitment and growth within themselves. Therefore, you, as your child's primary discipler, must take your relationship with Christ seriously so you can make a difference in the people God has given you. It is hard work! But the payoff is eternal.

Getting a Bigger Perspective

Ever heard these common phrases? "The apple doesn't fall far from the tree," "like father, like son," and "a chip off the old block." These illustrate the incredible comparisons between parents and their children. There are numerous similarities in looks, demeanors, and inclinations that can be uncanny. From a spiritual standpoint, however, it is astonishing to see the parallels in the parents' spiritual maturity levels and that of their children. In his book, *Parenting with Kingdom Purpose*, Ken Hemphill drove home this point when he said, "Most parents who want to know where their kids are headed religiously just need to look in the mirror."[5] This statement is so true. In many cases, the spiritual levels of the parents and their kids are remarkably related.

The Bible is keenly aware of these similarities. Scripture says, "Make every effort to live in peace with everyone and to be holy; without holiness no one will see the Lord" (Heb. 12:14). God desires a relationship with you. This is not new news, is it? There is nothing more important in a believer's life than his or her personal relationship with the Lord. He calls His children to be holy. This truth is not only for you but also for your children as well. Permit me to be forward. Is it time to get serious about your personal relationship with the Lord, not just for yourself but also for your children? Your children's spiritual growth depends on it. Why do I say this? I say it because of the chilling reality from Hebrews. The writer said, "Without holiness no one will see the Lord" (Heb. 12:14b).

God has deliberately placed each child in your life. They are no mistake. His goal is for you to prepare them to live out each day to honor Him. Discipleship with every child begins at home. God's design is to have every child living with the most influential people in their lives to constantly talk with them concerning God, help them properly think about God, and show them how to carefully obey God. In the end, you are ultimately responsible for preparing them for eternity. Let that sink in! Therefore, if children, especially teenagers, are ever going to experience a healthy relationship with the Lord, they need you to be running after God first. In other words, "It all starts with you!"

Needless to say, this is a serious matter. You can ill afford to take growing in your faith for granted. You must faithfully be a continual learner of the Word of God and deliberately live it out with consistency. Scott McConnell observed, "Students are experts at noticing inconsistencies between what parents say and do."[6] It is easy for parents to talk the talk, but the real issue comes down to can they walk the walk. Norma Schmidt stated,

> My mother had put her finger on an essential truth: Kids absorb the values they see adults putting into action. Ever notice how quickly kids spot any inconsistency between what we say and what we do? Long before kids can spell "hypocrisy," they notice when our actions fall short of our words. "Don't worry that children never listen to you; worry that they are always watching you," author Robert Fulghum says. Kids need to see us "walking the talk." In fact, we teach kids best when we practice "being what we want to see" in them.[7]

John Maxwell put it another way when he said, "we teach what we know, we reproduce what we are."[8] By and large, what you think about subjects, your attitude regarding situations, what you say concerning issues, and how you respond to circumstances often get adopted by your children. Christian Smith in his book *Soul Searching,* stated, "We'll get what we are. By normal processes of socialization, and unless other significant forces intervene, more than what parents might say they want as religious outcomes in their children, most parents most likely will end up getting religiously of their children what they themselves are."[9] Running after God may require you to make major adjustments in your thoughts, words, and actions. Parents, you need to focus all your attention on your own personal pursuit of God. The bottom line is this: you reproduce yourself in your kids whether you like it or not.

Hit Heaven Running

Parents have an enormous job to do. They are busy inside and outside the home. Nonetheless, God expects parents to pursue a growing personal relationship. Parents may ask, "How do you run after God in this day and time?" God has the answer. He desires His followers to pursue Him through His Word. God does not expect perfection but persistence. We trip, stumble, and fall; but getting back up and on the right track is what counts. Your pursuit may require adjustments in lifestyle, priorities, and mindset. Whatever the case, God expects parents to chase after Him at all costs.

Living for God begins with reading God's Word. There is no substitute. According to Lifeway, "the No. 1 catalyst for spiritual growth is simple: daily Bible reading."[10] In 2 Timothy 3:16-17 the Bible says, "All Scripture is God-breathed and is useful for teaching, rebuking, correcting and training in righteousness, so that the servant of God may be thoroughly equipped for every good work." Christ expects His followers to read their Bibles and pursue vibrant and healthy relationships with Him. Sounds simple, right? This unfortunately is not the case. A local survey was conducted that revealed a disturbing result in the homes of many Christian parents. Moms and dads of teenagers were asked, "During an average week, how many days do you read your Bible?" Only 34%[11] said they read their

Bible 5 to 7 times per week. In addition, a national survey conducted by Brad Waggoner uncovered some alarming statistics. He discovered, "Only 16 percent of Protestant churchgoers read their Bible daily and another 20 percent read it 'a few times a week.'"[12] Even though the Bible is the most popular book sold in the world, it appears that it is also the most neglected. This information points out a major disconnect. If Bible reading produces spiritual growth then that only means one thing! Parents must not be growing spiritually. Does this describe you? Does this disturb you? Christians seem to be short-circuiting the process. John Maxwell has said, "We cannot lead anyone else farther than we have been ourselves. Too many times we are so concerned about the product we try to shortcut the process."[13] It is time to stop the cycle. When parents shortcut the process of learning and growing in their own walks, the child is the ultimate loser. Parents, you must be determined to pursue a love relationship with the Lord. In other words, run after God with all you've got. You are qualified.

When I was a boy, my best friend Steve and I were at the local city pool. This was the largest pool in town complete with a slide, two small diving boards and one very high, high dive. I had never jumped off the high dive before basically because I was a big chicken. However on this day, Steve was daring me to try. Needless to say, I was scared to death. When I finally got up the nerve, I slowly climbed to the top of the ladder and made my way to the edge of the board. Just as I looked over the edge and saw how far from the water I was, I decided I was not ready to take the plunge. As I turned to make my way back down the ladder, there were already four or five people standing on the ladder waiting on me to get out of their way. I realized I was stuck and the only way down was to jump. I looked at Steve and he smiled and said, "just take off running." With nowhere to go except into the water I did what he said. I started running. However, I forgot to do one thing. I forgot to dive. When my feet left the diving board, I just kept running until I slammed into the water, face first. When I made it to the side of the pool, Steve was speechless. He couldn't talk because he was laughing so hard. When he finally pulled himself together he said, "You looked like a cartoon character running off the high dive. Your legs never stopped moving."

Here's the point. You and I have a short time on this planet to get to know God the Father, God the Son, and God the Spirit. From the moment we give our lives to Christ, God expects us to learn about Him through His written Word. However, there is coming a day when we will leave this earth. On that day, our earthly learning will be over, but our eternal learning will just be getting started. God wants us to run into His arms now and at death leap into His arms for the rest of eternity. I don't know about you, but I want to make the most of my time now and get to know my Redeemer the best I can so when my life is over I will hit heaven running.

Home Apps

Before you sit down to dinner tonight write out Hebrews 12:14a on index cards for everyone in your family. Write out "Make every effort to live in peace with everyone." While you're eating, have everyone give his or her interpretation of the verse. Then ask each person to describe how the verse was actually applied in his or her life recently. This is a great and simple way to show your family how the Bible can be lived out on a daily basis.

Day 7

But one thing I do: Forgetting what is behind and straining toward what is ahead, I press on toward the goal to win the prize for which God has called me heavenward in Christ Jesus. (Phil. 3:13b-14)

"'What' and 'if' two words as nonthreatening as words come. But put them together side-by-side and they have the power to haunt you for the rest of your life: 'What if?'..." Quote from the movie Letters to Juliet

Do you remember the time you met that special someone?

One day after gym class my friend David asked me what I was doing Friday night. I had already made plans to go to a movie with a friend named Sara from another school. He said, "Well if you get a chance I want to invite you to my surprise 16th birthday party." I asked, "Did you say surprise birthday party?" He replied, "Yeah, my mom's planning this big get-together for me and she's tried to keep it a secret, but that's not possible. Will you come?" I was telling him I wasn't sure I could when he said, "Remember the picture of that girl I showed you in science class the other day?" I said, "Of course I do, she was beautiful." Then he said, "She'll be there." That made me much more interested, but I didn't know what to do.

When Friday night came I went over to Sara's house, picked her up, and went to the movies. We had a good time, but her mom and dad expected her home right after the movie. When we got to her house, the lights were out and her parents were already in bed. I felt a little uncomfortable about sticking around even though it wasn't even ten o'clock yet. I decided to go to David's "surprise" party. As I drove, I was getting very excited about meeting that girl in the picture. When I got there I could not believe how deceived I was by David's picture. She was more beautiful than I expected. I joined in with the things going on at the party, but I wasn't able to bring myself to even speak to the girl in the picture. But one thing was for sure: I really wanted to get to know her even though I was too chicken to make eye contact. The next week in science class David came up and asked, "What did you think of the party?" I told him, "It was good, but your picture doesn't do that girl justice." He said, "I thought you might like her. How about I set you up with her and we'll double date?" I was beside myself. I couldn't believe he would do that for me so I quickly said, "Yes!" I really wanted to spend some time with her and get to know her. Then I asked, "Would you mind letting me have that picture?" That was over thirty years ago. I'm not sure what ever happened to that picture, but I know one thing: I haven't stopped spending time with that girl in the picture because she's now my wife. Just like I wanted to spend some time with that girl in the picture, God wants to spend time with you.

God's Obsession

God is obsessed in wanting a relationship with you. He is consumed with the thought of being with you not just right now but forever. He went to the greatest length possible to make that happen. God put His own Son on a cross over 2,000 years ago to die just to make a relationship with you possible. You may feel your relationship with the Lord is non-existent, cold, or distant. Maybe you're a parent who has never been to church much or has not been lately. On the other hand, perhaps you are enjoying a growing relationship with the Lord and you're plugged-in and engaged in a local church. No matter what your relationship status is, there are times when we all feel there are barriers between God and us. There is a tendency for people who are disengaged from God to think that He is out of reach. However, there is nothing God won't do on His end to break down and eliminate all barriers between Him and the ones He loves so much…especially when the barrier is from sin.

Barriers

God hates sin. However, God has made a way back to Him. For His children, He is ready and willing to reengage. The Bible says in 1 John 1:9, "If we confess our sins, He is faithful and just and will forgive us our sins and purify us from all unrighteousness." In order for followers of Christ to properly confess their sins, believers must agree with God that there is sin in their lives. Genuinely ask God to forgive you and be determined to say no to that sin again. Then, as a result, the Bible says, "He is faithful and just and will forgive us our sins" (1 Jn. 1:9b). No matter what the sin is, God wants to "forgive us our sins and purify us from all unrighteousness" (1 Jn. 1:9c).

King David was not a perfect man. Not by a long shot. Even though the Bible says, "God testified concerning him: 'I have found David son of Jesse, a man after my own heart...'" (Acts 13:22a) he had a major moral failure. David committed adultery with Bathsheba, got her pregnant, and then had her husband killed to try to cover up the whole mess. Many months went by before Nathan confronted King David concerning his sin. During that time his life was miserable. When David came to the end of his rope, he knew he needed to come clean before God. David said, "I acknowledged my sin to you and did not cover up my iniquity. I said, 'I will confess my transgressions to the Lord.' And you forgave the guilt of my sin" (Ps. 32:5).

Did you notice the word David used to describe the backwash of his sin? Guilt. In this context, God used guilt to bring David to his senses. This was a good thing. However, many times people have a hard time letting go of guilt, even after they have been forgiven. When we as believers authentically ask for God's forgiveness, we tend to still let that sin linger in our minds. Oftentimes we let sin have a residual effect. There's nothing healthy about that. Guilt makes us feel unworthy of God's forgiveness. Guilt keeps us bound to that sin. Guilt never lets us truly experience the freedom that forgiveness actually supplies. Satan loves to see us wallow in our mud puddle of guilt. Therefore, it's important to know what God does once we have sought His forgiveness. In other words, how does God handle our sin after we genuinely confess? The Bible says,

> For as high as the heavens are above the earth, so great is His love for those who fear Him; as far as the east is from the west, so far has He removed our transgressions from us. (Ps. 103:11-12)

> "Come now, let us settle the matter," says the Lord. "Though your sins are like scarlet, they shall be as white as snow; though they are red as crimson, they shall be like wool." (Isa. 1:18)

> For I will forgive their wickedness and will remember their sins no more. (Jer. 31:34b)

> You will again have compassion on us; you will tread our sins underfoot and hurl all our iniquities into the depths of the sea. (Mic. 7:19)

Listen carefully to these words. Let them sink in and soak into your soul. "As far as the east is from the west" (Ps. 103:12a). How far is that? "Your sins are like scarlet, they shall be as white as snow; though they are red as crimson, they shall be like wool" (Isa. 1:18b). Sin stains us, but God's forgiveness totally cleanses us. "I will…remember their sins no more" (Jer. 31:34b). This is beautiful. God chooses to forget. Permanent amnesia. I have no idea how He does that. But God is able to, "hurl all our iniquities into the depths of the sea" (Mic. 7:19b). In ancient times the sea was considered a place of death. God throws away our sin into a place of death. There is nothing God wouldn't do for you. He loves and cares for you and never wants sin to control you. God doesn't want the guilt that comes along with sin to enslave you.

A little boy and his sister always looked forward to their summers visiting their grandparents. When they arrived, the children always knew their grandfather had a special gift to give them. This summer was no exception. Greg received his first slingshot from his granddad. He loved playing with his new toy. He practiced and practiced, but he could never hit a thing. One day he went into the backyard of his grandparents house and saw his grandmother's pet duck. Without even thinking he loaded the slingshot, took aim, and shot at the duck. Incredibly, the stone hit the duck and it fell dead. Greg panicked. He desperately tried to hide the dead duck under a storage building, only to look up and see his sister Stacey watching. She had seen the whole thing but didn't say a word.

After lunch that day, Grandma said, "Stacey, how about we clean up and wash the dishes?" But Stacey said, "Grandma, Greg told me he wanted to help out in the kitchen today. Isn't that right, Greg?" Then she looked at him and whispered, "Remember the duck?" So Greg reluctantly helped his grandmother clean up and wash the dishes.

Later Grandpa asked the children if they wanted to go fishing. Grandma said, "I don't know if we'll have time to go because I need Stacey to help make dinner." Stacey grinned and said, "No problem. Greg will stay back and help you, Grandma. He wants to do it." Again she whispered, "Remember the duck?" Greg fumed and reluctantly stayed back while Stacey went fishing with Grandpa. This went on for days. Stacey was in full control. Several days went by with Greg doing both his and Stacey's chores. Finally, he had enough. He went to his grandma and confessed to her that he'd killed her duck. She looked Greg in the eyes and said, "I know you did" as she gave him a hug. "I was standing at the window and saw the whole thing happen. Greg, I love you and I forgave you. But I was wondering, why did you let Stacey make a slave out of you?"

Satan loves to use guilt to make a slave out of you. What if you said "No, I will not be a slave to guilt any longer?" What if you let Christ have you? What if you accept His complete forgiveness? What if you decide to live in His freedom? What if you decide to forget "what is behind and straining toward what is ahead" (Phil. 3:13b)? What if you believe the verse "if the Son sets you free, you will be free indeed" (Jn. 8:36). "What" and "if" are two words as nonthreatening as words come. But put them together side-by-side and they have the power to free you for the rest of your life…

Home Apps

Before dinner tonight, see if you can find a few Christmas cards you received last year. (If you've thrown them away, find cards that were sent to you on another occasion or list some of your neighbors that live nearby.) Just before you start eating, take two or three of the cards or names and pray for them individually. Why go to all this trouble? Often when guilt has enslaved us, we can get a little inwardly focused. This is a great exercise to help get you and your family to focus on others.

Day 8

To the angel of the church in Laodicea write:

These are the words of the Amen, the faithful and true witness, the ruler of God's creation. I know your deeds, that you are neither cold nor hot. I wish you were either one or the other! So, because you are lukewarm—neither hot nor cold—I am about to spit you out of my mouth. You say, 'I am rich; I have acquired wealth and do not need a thing.' But you do not realize that you are wretched, pitiful, poor, blind and naked. I counsel you to buy from me gold refined in the fire, so you can become rich; and white clothes to wear, so you can cover your shameful nakedness; and salve to put on your eyes, so you can see. Those whom I love I rebuke and discipline. So be earnest and repent. Here I am! I stand at the door and knock. If anyone hears my voice and opens the door, I will come in and eat with that person, and they with me. To the one who is victorious, I will give the right to sit with me on my throne, just as I was victorious and sat down with my Father on His throne. Whoever has ears, let them hear what the Spirit says to the churches. (Rev. 3:14-22)

"It's tiring to run from God. Perhaps you sense that He's pursuing you. If you do, it's time to stop running."
— Haddon W. Robinson

Are you ever out of God's reach?

When you were a kid, did you grow up watching 'Sesame Street?' If you did, I'm sure you'll remember the skinny, furry, blue character with the big red nose. Often he would introduce himself by saying, "Hello there. This is your old pal Grover." In one particular skit, Grover wanted to talk about the words "near" and "far." Grover always wanted his audience to learn new things. He would do almost anything to make sure he got his message across. Grover began by saying, "Today, I'm going to talk to you about near and far. In fact I, little furry Grover, am going to show you near and far. OK, here goes. First, this is near." Then he took a short step backward and stomped his feet. After making his point, he turned around and ran backwards about twenty paces. He spun around, stomped his feet again, and yelled, "This is farrrrr" in typical Grover fashion. He quickly ran toward the camera, now a little out of breath, and announced, "This is near." For a moment, Grover thinks he has taught the difference between the two words. With pride he feels he has effectively communicated and everybody watching understands the idea. However, he realizes that everyone has not understood his teaching. So Grover decides to repeat the process all over again. Grover has to repeat the running back and forth process five different times. With each repetition, he gets increasingly frustrated and more and more winded. By the end, Grover is completely discouraged and fatigued. He realizes he has failed and collapses from exhaustion.

Grover worked hard to make his point. He clearly taught us the meanings of the words near and far. When it comes to a relationship with Christ, God always wants us near not far. In the book of Revelation, Jesus confronts the church of Laodicea with the fact they have distanced themselves from Him. At one time the church was growing and trusting in the Lord for everything. They were enjoying a close relationship with Christ. But something happened to change that closeness. Jesus speaks to the church and says, "I know your deeds, that you are neither cold nor hot. I wish you were either one or the other! So, because you are lukewarm—neither hot nor cold—I am about to spit you out of my mouth" (Rev. 3:15-16). We often read these words and assume Jesus doesn't want His followers to be fence riders. Many people read these verses and take them to mean Jesus either wants people to be "hot" or "cold" for Him. When you think about it, is that what He really means? I can see being "hot" for Jesus but I'm not sure what being "cold" for Jesus looks like. Actually, it doesn't fit.

Before we can completely understand this passage we have to know a few things about Laodicea's history and landscape. Laodicea was a small but financially-secure community. The city was well known for two particular items of trade. Laodicea had great wealth because of a thriving textile industry and the production of an eye ointment with healing properties. As these products flourished, their wealth increased. However, as their cash flow grew, their independence grew as well. On the surface, things could not be better. But Laodicea had a major problem that had nothing to do with their commerce. Their water was polluted. But to the Laodiceans, this was not a problem. That's why they could boastfully say, "I am rich; I have acquired wealth and do not need a thing" (Rev. 3:17). In other words, they had no intentions of seeking the Lord when they had problems.

They could handle anything. If they had a problem, all they needed to do was to throw money at it. And that's exactly what they did.

First, let's get an idea of the landscape. Located approximately 3½ miles away from Laodicea were two towns that could solve their water pollution problem. Colosse, just east of Laodicea, was a town well known for their refreshing cold-water springs. What is better to drink on a hot day or after working hard making cloth than a nice cold glass of water? Hierapolis, just north of Laodicea, was a town well known for their soothing natural hot-water springs. After a hard day's work of making eye-cream there is nothing better than to relax in a hot tub of water, letting the heat rejuvenate your tired and aching muscles. The solution was simple. All they had to do was buy the cold water from Colosse and the hot water from Hierapolis. Their plan was flawless. Except for one thing. Both water sources were still 3½ miles away. To many people of that day, getting water 3½ miles would be insurmountable, but not to the Laodiceans. They had a brilliant idea. Since they were independent and wealthy, they would just throw their money at the problem. So what did they do? They built two pipelines. The Laodiceans constructed one pipeline from Colosse for the refreshing cold water and another pipeline from Hierapolis for the soothing hot water.

The people of Laodicea were elated. Now they could solve their polluted water problem and go on enjoying life. Who needs God when you're smart, industrious, and wealthy? After all the pipeline construction was complete, the day finally came for the Laodiceans to enjoy their cold and hot water from the tap. However, when they turned on the faucets, they were shocked to find out their plan had failed. There was no cold water. There was no hot water. The water from both sources was 'lukewarm.' All that time and money was spent to only bring disappointment. Why? Why was the water lukewarm? There is a simple explanation. By the time the cold water from Colosse traveled the 3½ miles to Laodicea the water temperature changed from cold to lukewarm. By the time the hot water from Hierapolis traveled the 3½ miles to Laodicea the water temperature changed from hot to lukewarm. Laodicea was too far away from the water sources.

Have you ever been hot and thirsty and walked up to a water fountain needing a nice cold drink of water? When you turn the knob and lower your mouth to get a sip of that liquid refreshment, you find that the water fountain is broken or unplugged because the water is lukewarm. What is the first thing most people do? They spit it out! That's why Jesus said, "So, because you are lukewarm—neither hot nor cold—I am about to spit you out of my mouth" (Rev. 3:16). Bottom line, the Laodiceans were too far away from the source. They had distanced themselves from God. Jesus was speaking directly into their hearts and giving them a "3 D" illustration of their true condition. Their money, prestige, and independence separated them from the Lord. They were blinded by their pride.

However, Jesus never has nor will He ever leave us alone in our failure. He always offers His children redemption. He always makes the way back to Him possible. Jesus points this out to His wayward children when He says, "I counsel you to buy from me gold refined in the fire, so you can become rich; and white clothes to wear, so you can cover your shameful nakedness; and salve to put on your eyes, so you can see" (Rev. 3:18). Jesus always makes a way back for us to have a relationship with Him. His love is real. That's why He says, "Those whom I love I rebuke and discipline. So be earnest and repent" (Rev. 3:19). It is never too late. There is always hope. Jesus wants to restore your relationship with Him. He wants to be close to you and wants you close to Him. He's the God of second chances. He wants to make it better than it ever was before. He is ready to start fresh with you. Jesus says, "Here I am! I stand at the door and knock. If anyone hears my voice and opens the door, I will come in and eat with that person, and they with me" (Rev. 3:20). You may be thinking you are too far away from Christ and it's too late. That simply is not true. You are never too far from God. You may feel you've been independent for so long God no longer wants a relationship with you. Jesus is knocking. He's calling out to you. Open the door. Let Him come in. Restart your relationship with the Savior right now and allow Him to be victorious in your life.

When I was a little boy, one of my favorite parts of the day was when our family sat down together to watch television. I would come in from playing outside, eat dinner, and get my bath. Then the entire family would eventually make their way into the den to watch our favorite shows. Back then we were watching the first episodes of shows like "All in the Family," "Star Trek," and "I Love Lucy" on one of only three local channels. My favorite place to sit and watch television was in my dad's lazy-boy recliner. My mom had her chair. My sister was on the couch and my brother on the floor while Daddy and I were sitting in the recliner. I would sit in his chair along with him. Side-by-side we sat in the recliner together. We sat so close together that I could hear every breath he took. I can even remember how he smelled.

Those were days I will never forget. Unfortunately, I'm not able to sit in too many chairs with anybody these days. I think recliners have gotten smaller. I'm not sure. Nevertheless, I am looking forward to the day that I'll get to sit in a chair with my Savior. How about you? According to the Scripture, we have a special invitation from Jesus. The Bible says, "To the one who is victorious, I will give the right to sit with me on my throne, just as I was victorious and sat down with my Father on his throne" (Rev. 3:21). Now that's something I'm looking forward to.

Home Apps

Is there a place near your home you like to go that helps you feel closer to the Lord? Before the day is out, make an appointment with yourself. Get your planner out and within the next seven days schedule a time to slip away alone. Only take your Bible. Spend some time reading any of your favorite verses, a passage you've heard preached lately, or just pick something random. The goal is to get one-on-one with God to 'draw near' to Him.

Day 9

Therefore, holy brothers and sisters, who share in the heavenly calling, fix your thoughts on Jesus… (Heb. 3:1)

"A recent study proves that, when it comes to bringing up children, more is caught than taught."
— Mary Rettig

What holds you back?

What if I told you the world is flat? You wouldn't buy it, nor would I. However, if you lived back before the 15th century there would be no question in your mind that the world was a frisbee. No one challenged this thinking until Christopher Columbus came along. He was not convinced of the so-called experts' rationale. In 1492 he went to the king and queen of Spain and asked for ships, money, and men to disprove the idea that the earth was flat. The crown granted his request, and as you know, "the rest is history." But have you ever wondered where Columbus got the bright idea that the planet was a ball and not a disk? God told him. In Isaiah 40:22 the Bible says, "He sits enthroned above the circle of the earth, and its people are like grasshoppers." The word circle literally means, "sphere." The power of Scripture altered the thinking of humanity. For over 7,000 years people believed we lived on a pancake. For over 7,000 years people were afraid to venture too far from the safety of land in fear of going over the edge and falling off the world. One idea. One belief. One thought kept people captive for thousands of years. That's a new perspective of how powerful thoughts can be.

The Power of Thoughts

Our thoughts are indeed powerful. The things we think are the very foundation of our lives. Our thoughts set the course and direction of our lives. It has been said,

- *Watch your thoughts; they become words.*
- *Watch your words; they become actions.*
- *Watch your actions; they become habits.*
- *Watch your habits; they become character.*
- *Watch your character; it becomes your destiny.*[14]

Notice the sequence? That's why God has much to say about His children's thoughts. As a matter of fact, Jesus doesn't hesitate to talk about the importance of our thoughts.

One day, while Jesus was preaching on the Mount of Olives, He made the statement, "You have heard that it was said, 'You shall not commit adultery.' But I tell you that anyone who looks at a woman lustfully has already committed adultery with her in his heart" (Matt. 5:27-28). You may be saying, "Well I'm safe on this one; I've never done anything like that." Let's take a closer look at this. Notice how Jesus interprets His statement. He used the word "looks" as the action word. He didn't use the word say or act. Jesus specifically said "looks." Then to top it all off He follows that up with the phrase "adultery with her in his heart" (Matt. 5:28b). That's a pretty serious sin. Jesus reaches all the way back into the Old Testament to get that one out and for good reason. Notice that when you put those two together you don't have to move a muscle to commit adultery. You don't have to be in any particular place. You don't have to be doing any specific activity. As a matter of fact, you can have lustful thoughts in the confines of your own head. As a result, no one would ever know about it except you and the Lord. Basically, Jesus is pointing out how simple it is to sin with only your thoughts. Now that is powerful.

There are several verses and passages in God's Word that help us understand the importance of controlling our thoughts. The Bible says, "We demolish arguments and every pretension that sets itself up against the knowledge of God, and we take captive every thought to make it obedient to Christ" (2 Cor. 10:5). If we don't take our thoughts captive, it could lead to inappropriate words, actions, and habits and could ultimately be displayed in our character. Wrong thoughts have the potential to lead us down a path that will affect our entire lives. That's why the Bible says, "Set your minds on things above, not on earthly things" (Col. 3:2). God desires for His followers to put Him first in every aspect of their lives, especially their thinking, because thoughts have power.

The Power of Words

The words we use flow naturally from our thoughts. Words that are spoken have the ability to promote the most good or cause the most damage. Scripture spends a great deal of time addressing the words we use. Once again Jesus said, "For the mouth speaks what the heart is full of" (Matt. 12:34b). Jesus was saying people talk about what their hearts are filled with. After that statement the Lord said something startling. He said, "But I tell you that everyone will have to give account on the Day of Judgment for every empty word they have spoken" (Matt. 12:36). Let that sink in for a minute. Jesus is simply saying that every person will have to explain the intention of every word they ever used when they stand before God. That's big. James, the half brother of Jesus, also said, "Those who consider themselves religious and yet do not keep a tight rein on their tongues deceive themselves, and their religion is worthless" (Jas. 1:26). God takes seriously the words people use. People can tell if faith is real for a person just by listening to the words that person speaks. Every word is important. As a result, parents who have the most authority in a child's life must take special care regarding the use of all words. When parents fail to use words appropriately, they give their kids permission to follow their example.

The Bible says in Colossian 3:8, "But now you must also rid yourselves of all such things as these...filthy language from your lips." Christian parents need to consider every word that is spoken in their homes. Slang words, crude speech, filthy language, and dirty jokes have no place in a believer's life. Children are very quick to imitate words and phrases their parents use. Parents need to understand when they use impure words and phrases they are giving their children permission to do the same.

Let's take it one step further. Kids can interpret exaggeration, not fulfilling promises, and not telling the truth as acceptable behavior. When children hear their parents embellishing stories, not keeping promises, or giving false information, it causes confusion in their minds. The Bible says, "Do not lie to each other, since you have taken off your old self with its practices" (Col. 3:9). Many children instinctively know it is wrong to lie. Parents must set the right standards and examples in their homes. When parents do not keep a promise or stretch the truth, they are giving permission to their children to copy their behavior. Remember, more is caught than taught.

Words are powerful! Paul said, "But now you must also rid yourselves of all such things as these: anger, rage, malice, slander, and filthy language from your lips" (Col. 3:8). When Christian parents use words in anger, have a critical spirit, or shout in a loud voice or a harsh tone, it can cause a number of problems. Parents can make their kids feel unworthy, timid, insecure, and self-conscious when they speak toward them in these ways. Parents should never tear down people. They are commanded to "Encourage one another and build each other up" (1 Thess. 5:11). That's why the Bible pleads with every believer, especially parents, to, "Get rid of all bitterness, rage and anger, brawling and slander, along with every form of malice" (Eph. 4:31). When parents fail to use words properly, they are giving consent to their kids to do the same. Parents need to control their speech and consider, "we teach kids best when we practice 'being what we want to see' in them."[15]

The Power of Actions

The old saying, "Actions speak louder than words" is too often extraordinarily true. Kids put parents' actions under a microscope whenever they get an opportunity. They are constantly watching for consistency and authenticity. At the same time, they are also looking for someone to imitate. A Christian parent's behavior should constantly take on exemplary characteristics.

Paul, when he spoke to the believers in Corinth, said, "So whether you eat or drink or whatever you do, do it all for the glory of God" (1 Cor. 10:31). In the context of this verse, Paul was reminding the more mature believers of the church that they needed to be a good example to the Jews, Greeks, and new followers of Jesus Christ. In other words, he was commanding the established believers to display proper behavior especially when they were among people who opposed their beliefs, were indifferent, or were younger believers. Paul clearly encourages parents to exhibit proper actions no matter where they are. As parents interact with the community, friends, and family, they are to do it in such a way that it will bring honor to God. Children want to hear and see the lives of their parents match God's standards for life because as it turns out "we teach what we know, we reproduce what we are."[16]

Paul instructed fellow believers in their conduct. In chapter 3 of Colossians, he encouraged Christians to allow Christ to rule them, to be thankful for what God had done in their lives, to let the Word live in them, and to edify Christ and the church. He capped off his commands when he said, "And whatever you do, whether in word or deed, do it all in the name of the Lord Jesus, giving thanks to God the Father through Him" (Col. 3:17). For Christians, no matter what they say or do, it should be considered an action to and for the Lord. William Barclay put it another way when he said, "One of the best tests of any action is: Can a person do it calling upon the name of Jesus? Can he do it while asking for His help? A good test for what is spoken is: Can one speak it and, in the same breath, name the name of the Lord Jesus? Can one speak it remembering that Jesus will hear, or asking Him to hear?"[17] Every action has to be connected to the name of Jesus Christ. In any situation a Christian parent's action does not match the Bible, a child sees an opportunity to compromise. Parents can ill afford to negotiate in this area. There can be no concession made to this command. Paul lived out this command in his life, and he encouraged parents to do the same today. That is why he was able to say, "I urge you to imitate me" (1 Cor. 4:16). Children want to hear and see the lives of their parents match the Word of God because they are looking for someone to model life for them.

God's Solution

I know the discussion today has been a boatload of stuff. But let's take a step back. It's possible you've felt a little overwhelmed by some of the things mentioned. You may be saying, "Every day I see my daughter having the same thoughts about herself that I do. I hear my son using the same words and phrases I use, good and bad, all the time. I'm always amazed at how my children imitate their other parent's actions. The problem is I don't know how to control my thoughts, words, and actions. How does a busy parent pull all this together? Is it possible?" The simple answer is yes. But it can only be done one way, and that's through God's Word.

In the book of Proverbs the wisest man who ever lived said, "Above all else, guard your heart, for everything you do flows from it" (Prov. 4:23). Notice how the wisest man understood everything you do flows from the heart. That means your thoughts, words, and actions all flow from your heart. It really is a heart issue. Do you need something done to your heart? Let me ask, are you ready for God to do heart surgery? Are you willing to let Him remove the darkness of your past that has caused you so much pain? Will you let the Lord repair the damage that hurt has caused and scarred you so deeply? Can you give God access to the broken areas of your life that you've tried to mask over and keep hidden away? These are the things that have been accumulating over the years and is causing so much turmoil in your life now. Why do you hold on to these things? Is it really worth it? Look at it through the eyes of your children and ask that same question again. Isn't it time to release the pain, hurt, and brokenness of the past and start fresh? If not now, then when? Your kids need this almost as much as you do.

Home Apps

Today we discussed the tremendous power of our thoughts, words, and actions. Here's a mental exercise that will take some serious concentration and effort on your part. The Bible says in 1 Thessalonians 5:11, "Therefore encourage one another and build each other up." Either today or tomorrow intentionally set aside the day to live out this verse. As you go through your day, find a way to encourage, compliment, or express adoration to every person you speak to. The reason is simple. This will help you focus your thoughts, be uplifting with your words, and display loving and caring actions to other people.

Day 10

But grow in the grace and knowledge of our Lord and Savior Jesus Christ. To Him be glory both now and forever! Amen. (2 Pet. 3:18)

"If your vision is for a year, plant wheat.
If your vision is for ten years, plant trees.
If your vision is for a lifetime, plant people."
— Chinese Proverb

What do you dream for your children?

Bill Hybels, pastor of Willow Creek Community Church, tells this story in his book *Who You Are When No One's Looking*. He wrote,

> *It started like so many evenings. Mom and Dad at home and Jimmy playing after dinner. Mom and dad were absorbed with jobs and did not notice the time. It was a full moon and some of the light seeped through the windows. Then mom glanced at the clock. "Jimmy, it's time to go to bed. Go up now and I'll come and settle you later." Unlike usual, Jimmy went straight upstairs to his room. An hour or so later his mother came up to check if all was well, and to her astonishment found that her son was staring quietly out of his window at the moonlit scenery. "What are you doing, Jimmy?" "I'm looking at the moon, Mommy." "Well, it's time to go to bed now." As one reluctant boy settled down, he said, "Mommy, you know one day I'm going to walk on the moon." Who could have known that the boy in whom the dream was planted that night would survive a near fatal motorbike crash which broke almost every bone in his body, and would bring to fruition this dream 32 years later when James Irwin stepped on the moon's surface, just one of the 12 representatives of the human race to have done so?[18]*

Dreams are powerful. What dreams do you have for your children in the future? In other words, what is your vision for them? I don't mean what sport you want them to play. I'm not talking about what college they attend. Nor am I saying anything about the profession you want them to have. That's small stuff. Dream big. I'm referring to things much larger. Eternal things. Let me ask the question another way: What is your "kingdom vision" for your children?

One day we will all stand before the Lord. The Bible says in Romans 14:12, "each of us will give an account of ourselves to God." That's a sobering thought. There are many areas of my life I am not looking forward to discussing with God. However, there is one part of my life I want to work hard at and do my best now because I know that the "give an account" (Rom. 14:12) day is coming. Raising my children is that area. As a matter of fact, I would venture to say it is an important area in your life too. On the day I meet Jesus face to face, I want to hear Him say, "Well done, good and faithful servant" (Mt. 25:21). For that to happen, I know I need to seek God's face now more than ever to see what He desires for my children. But even before that, I know my relationship with the Lord has to come first. What about you?

Vision

What is vision? John Maxwell is one of my favorite authors and speakers. He is one of those men I allow to speak into my life. Maxwell is a man full of wisdom and experience. I go to him for godly counsel on just about any subject, especially when it comes to vision. He has said:

- *Vision is foresight with insight based on hindsight.*
- *Vision is seeing the invisible and making it visible.*
- *Vision is an informed bridge from the present to a better future.*
- *Vision is a picture held in your mind's eye of the way things could or should be in the days ahead.*
- *Vision connotes a visual reality, a portrait of a preferred future.*[19]

Vision is important. Allow me to be a little bold and ask some tough questions. Would you like to see each of your children ask Christ into their lives? Do you want to see them living out their faith in a way that God would be happy with? How about seeing them in heaven one day and living with them for all eternity? I'm going to assume you said "yes" to each of these questions. Can you picture what that looks like? That's a kingdom vision. Now let me ask the boldest question of them all. What are you going to do today to make that future a reality? You cannot say yes to these questions and expect your kingdom vision to just happen. You have to begin today laying the foundation on Biblical principles and strategically build toward that kingdom vision each day. It takes making a decision, being determined, and going the distance.

Kingdom Vision Foundation

Let's go back over the last few days to build a secure kingdom vision foundation. We have to ask a simple but big question. Is it possible to grow in your relationship with Christ apart from the Bible? No, it is not. Without God's Word in your life, how are you going to lead anyone anywhere that you have never been?

Reading the Bible is not difficult, but it does take a decision. Have you ever been asked the question, "How do you eat an elephant?" The answer of course is "one bite at a time." That's exactly the same approach you should take when reading the Bible – one bite at a time. But you have to decide to start. Next it takes determination. Be determined that nothing is going to stop you from getting closer to God. Be determined that no matter what it takes, you are not going to let anything get in the way of your time with God. Make an appointment. Set a time and keep it. Finally, go the distance. Be in it for the long haul. Hit heaven running. You may slip, trip, or fall, but get back up and get back on track. The kingdom vision is worth it. Your child is worth it.

Over the years I have talked to numerous people about their relationships with the Lord. Too often I find many people running from God, not running to Him. By far, the number one reason why a person feels his relationship with the Lord is dead or drifting is because of sin. Temptation can get the best of us and, as a result, we give in to sin. As a follower of Christ, the Holy Spirit will not sit still for a minute. He begins to poke, prod, and pester you to get you to come clean with God. That's why the Bible says,

My son, do not make light of the Lord's discipline, and do not lose heart when He rebukes you, because the Lord disciplines the one He loves, and He chastens everyone He accepts as His son... God is treating you as His children. For what children are not disciplined by their father? If you are not disciplined—and everyone undergoes discipline—then you are not legitimate, not true sons and daughters at all. (Heb. 12:5b-6, 7b-8)

This may sound strange, but this is a good thing. God is showing His true love for you. He only wants the best for you. That's why the Holy Spirit is relentless. God wants to eradicate the sin from your life. God wants you to come to Him and agree that your sin is wrong according to His standard. Then He wants you to ask Him for forgiveness, accept His freedom, and give the Holy Spirit full control of your life. However, sometimes people short-circuit God's plan. They ask for forgiveness but hold on to the guilt of sin. In other words, they don't forgive themselves. Over time, a person can feel unworthy of God's freedom. As a result, a mountain of guilt buries them, and their relationship becomes stagnate and stale. Satan loves this. Have you ever felt that? Do you want your children to grow up this way? If guilt has drained you to the point you don't sense God anywhere, I've got great news for you.

God never intends for His children to live with the slightest amount of guilt. That's why it is so important for a follower of Christ to understand two very important truths about God: His forgiveness and forgetfulness. In 1 John 1:9 the Bible says, "If we confess our sins, He is faithful and just and will forgive us our sins and purify us from all unrighteousness." God says He will forgive genuinely confessed sin. No ifs, ands, or buts. Then God does four things with our confessed sin. He removes our sin as far as the east is from the west. He washes us as white as snow. He remembers our sin no more. God hurls our sin into the sea of forgetfulness. That is freedom. Decide today to take hold of this truth. Be determined to live in this truth. You need this and so do your children. And oh, by the way, if God has forgiven you, who are you to not forgive yourself?

Remember King David? The Bible says, "God testified concerning him: 'I have found David son of Jesse, a man after my own heart; he will do everything I want him to do'" (Acts 13:22b). Do you recall he was an adulterer, murderer, and a liar? Not only that, he was not the greatest father the world has ever known. But God made sure David would always be known as a man after His heart. Why do I bring him up again? Simple. No matter how far you fall away from God there is always hope. You have this hope. You and your children need for you to go the distance and live out this hope. That's what a kingdom vision foundation is built on.

One of Sherri's and my favorite restaurants is Carrabba's. We love to go without our children and spend time with one another. It's always a special night when we get to share a meal together at a place like that. Having a quiet meal together is one the most intimate things couples can do. To build a kingdom vision foundation for your children you need this same intimacy with the Lord. As a perfect gentleman, Christ quietly invites us to experience intimacy with Him. He is standing at your heart's door. He's softly knocking on your door, not beating it down. He's simply asking you to allow Him to come in and eat with you. Intimacy. James said, "Draw near to God, and He will draw near to you" (Jas 4:8). You may be thinking you are too far away from Christ and it's too late. That simply is not true. You are never too far from Him. You may feel you've been independent for so long God no longer wants a relationship with you. Wrong again! Jesus is softly and persistently knocking. He's calling out to you. You're His child. Open the door. Let Him in. Make the decision today to restart your relationship with the Savior. Allow Him to be victorious in your life. Then be determined to let your children see and experience you enjoying your relationship with the Lord.

To make sure you experience that victory in your life, there are some important things to consider. Stop letting your thoughts, words, and actions run wild in your life. Perhaps you need to make some changes. Changes are God's specialty. He always allows second chances. If you don't believe me, ask Abraham, Moses, David, Jonah, Peter, and Paul just to name a few. These were men who took advantage of God's offering. God then used them in extraordinary ways. Paul Harvey was asked by a radio commentator, "What is the secret to your success?" Harvey answered, "I get up when I fall down."[20] That's determination to go the distance. Kingdom visions are built on these principles. Building is hard work. Is it worth it to you?

Did you know you could buy a 12-inch bar of solid steel for $5? That may not be news to you, but let's just say you take the bar of steel and cut it into two pieces, heat them, and bend them into two horseshoes. The value of the $5 bar of steel is now worth $10. If you take the same $5 bar of steel you can cut, machine, and sharpen each piece to make ten knives. The value of the $5 bar of steel is now worth $50. Let's not stop there. Let's say you take the same $5 bar of steel and heat, press, roll, and cut the metal into 200 small thin pieces to make keys. Now the value of the $5 bar is worth $100. Consider taking a few more steps. If you heat, press, roll, and machine the steel with precision equipment, you can make the steel bar into 10,000 watch springs. That simple $5 bar of steel is now worth $500. What you do with the steel determines the worth. The more detailed the process, the more the worth goes up. How hard are you willing to work to get the most value from your kingdom vision?

Home Apps

We talked in Day 5 about having someone in your life that is an accountability partner, a mentor, or a life coach in spiritual things. In light of the last few days of reading let me ask a few personal questions. Do you have one yet? If you do, great! If not, are you seeking the Lord for guidance. Here's the reason I ask. The last five days of reading has had a lot to do with your personal relationship with the Lord. Having an accountability partner, mentor, or life coach can help in many ways keep you focused and on a positive growth track. Get with someone as soon as possible, and ask them to help you with the things you're struggling with. One day your kids will thank you.

SPIRITUAL LEADERSHIP
IN THE HOME

Read This First – Week 3 Intro...

Before high-rise buildings can have any chance of standing they must first have a solid foundation. The same principle applies to discipleship. Now that you see the importance of making your personal relationship with the Lord a priority, perhaps the phrase "we teach what we know, we reproduce what we are"[1] has a little different meaning.

This week's reading is going to be a transition. We will be taking what you've read over the last two weeks and putting these principles into action. Our journey will continue as we discuss what the Bible says about spiritual leadership in the home. More specifically, we'll explore ways to lead our families to God and into a deeper relationship with Him. As a parent, there is no greater responsibility. How we lead our family today has the potential to change the trajectory of our children's future. How far reaching is that? Only the Lord knows; however, spiritual leadership in the home is God's will for you. That's why it is so important that we take on this responsibility His way.

Once more He visited Cana in Galilee, where He had turned the water into wine. And there was a certain royal official whose son lay sick at Capernaum. When this man heard that Jesus had arrived in Galilee from Judea, he went to Him and begged Him to come and heal his son, who was close to death. "Unless you people see signs and wonders," Jesus told him, "you will never believe." The royal official said, "Sir, come down before my child dies." "Go," Jesus replied, "your son will live." The man took Jesus at His word and departed. While he was still on the way, his servants met him with the news that his boy was living. When he inquired as to the time when his son got better, they said to him, "Yesterday, at one in the afternoon, the fever left him." Then the father realized that this was the exact time at which Jesus had said to him, "Your son will live." So he and his whole household believed. This was the second sign Jesus performed after coming from Judea to Galilee. (Jn. 4:46-54)

"If you do not have enough time for your children you can be 100% certain you are not following God's will for your life."
— Rodney Cooper

Day 11

Come, my children, listen to me; I will teach you the fear of the Lord. (Ps. 34:11)

"To be in your children's memories tomorrow, you have to be in their lives today."
— Anonymous

How engaged are you with your kids?

Mike and Natalie, a very godly couple I had the privilege to marry several years ago, had been married for some time and could not wait to have a baby. Needless to say, when they found out they were expecting a boy they were very excited. During the nine-month anticipation process, Mike and Natalie busied themselves preparing the baby room. However, this was not a normal room prep. Mike was an avid New York Yankee Baseball fanatic and his son would be too…whether he liked it or not. They painted the new baby's room the official colors, navy blue and white. The décor reeked of Yankee logos and paraphernalia. The bedspread, wall border, pillows, trashcan, rocking chair, pictures, even the mobile hanging over the crib all paid tribute to the team. The place was a shrine to the Bronx Bombers. There was nothing in the room that the late George Steinbrenner would not have been proud of. Perhaps you can identify with Mike and Natalie and have a story that rivals their interior design prowess. On the other hand, maybe you feel like you did well just getting the baby's room put together before he or she arrived. Regardless, most would agree that room preparation projects are a distant second when compared to the mission God has given all parents. Even though Mike and Natalie's son will hopefully grow up to become a Red Sox fan, knowing his mom and dad's zealousness for Christ, he will live in a home that teaches about the Lord and His Son.

Mary and Joseph wanted to be awesome parents, just like Mike and Natalie. They desired to teach their son well. With all their hearts, they wanted to show Him how to properly enter into the presence of the Lord. They were determined to provide for Jesus everything He needed so He could grow into the man with whom the Heavenly Father would be pleased.

It's safe to say that Mary and Joseph did an excellent job in raising their son. With that said, we can learn a few things from these enormously blessed people. The Bible has little information regarding the childhood of Jesus; however, Luke sheds a small ray of light on the early life of Christ. The Bible says,

> *When Joseph and Mary had done everything required by the Law of the Lord, they returned to Galilee to their own town of Nazareth. And the child grew and became strong; He was filled with wisdom, and the grace of God was on Him. Every year His parents went to Jerusalem for the Feast of the Passover. When He was twelve years old, they went up to the Feast, according to the custom… After three days they found Him in the temple courts, sitting among the teachers, listening to them and asking them questions. Everyone who heard Him was amazed at His understanding. (Lk. 2:39-42, 46-47)*

Even though little is known about Jesus' adolescence, there are some important truths we can learn from these few short verses.

Mary and Joseph demonstrate how to scripturally "Train up a child in the way he should go" (Prov. 22:6a KJV). It is evident in these verses that Jesus' home life provided Him the ability to grow mentally and spiritually. Mary and Joseph did, "everything required by the Law of the Lord" (Lk. 2:39). As Jesus' parents, they were dedicated to properly teach their son about God and His Word. David Black said, "In Jewish thought, the highest goal of life is 'the knowledge of God.' All education was directed toward this end."[2] This truth is even more apparent in the Scriptures describing the trip to Jerusalem for the Passover when He was twelve years old. The feast was over, and the family and others began their long journey back to Nazareth. Once they discovered Jesus was missing from the caravan, Mary and Joseph returned to Jerusalem to find their son.

Before you turn Mary and Joseph over to Social Services, you have to remember that families would travel to these celebrations in mass quantities. It was a big party. Not only that, it was a safer way to travel. As a result, Jesus' mom and dad assumed their son was tagging along in the crowd. They had no reason to suspect otherwise. Besides, would you think you would have obedience problems with the Son of God?

Luke 2:46 says, "After three days they found Him in the temple courts, sitting among the teachers, listening to them and asking them questions." There are two very important things to consider from this event. First, Scripture portrays Jesus as having a hunger for spiritual things. He was found in the temple courts sitting, listening, and asking questions of the teachers. We can give some credit to Mary and Joseph for this action. They were obviously obedient to the requirements of the Law, the instructions given in the Shema, and Proverbs 22:6 as seen in their son's actions. Secondly, it is evident that Jesus had been taught subjects pertaining to Scripture by Mary and Joseph and perhaps others. In the later part of Luke 2 verse 47 says, "Everyone who heard Him was amazed at His understanding." The fact that He was with the teachers of the temple and had a conversation with them reveals that spiritual discussions were not foreign to Him. He engaged in a spiritual exchange with the teachers of the Law. Obviously, Jesus' parents were dedicated to properly teaching their young son the truths of Scripture.

Engaging in spiritual conversations with your children can be the most memorable, rewarding, and meaningful times in the life of your family. There are countless benefits from specifically spending time in God's Word and learning together as a family. You don't need a theological degree to talk about the Bible. Just talk about God. Bring up the latest sermon your pastor preached. Pick a verse to memorize and talk about it every day. Start a devotion time with your family once a week. There are numerous ways to get into God's Word, and each of them can be life changing. Don't believe me? Let's go to some experts. I caught up with a former student from my youth ministry. She and her husband have two pre-school children. I asked them what they do for devotion time with their little ones. Heather said,

> As far as family devotion time, we don't really do one as a whole family. But, every
> night before bedtime, John and I read to them out of their kid's Bibles. Since I home

school, as I teach the kids each week (preschool stuff) I incorporate a verse that we memorize. As we go through the week we find different ways to apply the verse.

Not long ago, a mom and dad were feeling a little disconnected from their teenage daughter. I challenged them to begin a family devotion time. I asked the mom recently how she and her husband were doing with their family devotions. Shannon said,

> *They are going well. …I really have enjoyed the closeness it brings to our family. I feel like we have grown from this. By the way, I just looked up a new devotion today on that website you gave me called www.dare2share.org. It is great!*

Do not underestimate the power of the Holy Spirit when you invite Him into the life of your family. The payback is eternal.

A godly mother once shared with me how she spends a few minutes in her daughter's room just before bedtime. She talks to her about her day and has a short devotion. Unfortunately, her husband doesn't see the importance or the need to have a devotion time so she goes at it alone.

In the book of Acts, the Bible talks about a lady named Lydia who was a successful businesswoman. She was known as a worshiper of God. In the passage, the Bible makes no mention of a husband or children. It's possible she was a widow and had children, but Scripture does not say. However, the Bible does say she put her faith and trust in Christ, and "she and the members of her household were baptized" (Acts 16:15a). This tells us a great deal about her leadership and influence on the people who lived with her. These could have been servants or relatives, but the point is that she was someone who led people to Christ. No matter what marital situation you find yourself in, the Lord expects you, as the parent, to train your child.

Another thing we see in Scripture is the dedication of Mary and Joseph to the commandments of God to attend the annual Passover celebration. In Deuteronomy 16:1 the Bible says, "Observe the month of Aviv and celebrate the Passover of the Lord your God, because in the month of Aviv He brought you out of Egypt by night." Jesus' parents were determined to give their son every opportunity to worship the Heavenly Father. In Luke 2:41-42 the Bible says, "Every year His parents went to Jerusalem for the Feast of the Passover. When He was twelve years old, they went up to the Feast, according to the custom." Each family member was to participate in the Passover celebration that was led by the father. Joseph made sure his son observed him leading the family into the presence of the Lord and interceding in prayer on their behalf. Joseph, as the head of the home, became his family's link to the Father during the celebration. This image would be a picture Jesus would later display in His own life.

What images are you instilling in the life of your family regarding worship? Are you leading your family in worship at home and to worship weekly? Mary and Joseph set the example and God desires us to follow in their footsteps. A number of studies indicate that the greater the priority parents give to spiritual matters with their children, the greater the chance they are to sustain a growing relationship with the Lord as adults. In other words, the habits you nurture today can and oftentimes do carry on when they are out on their own.

Incidentally, there is one more thing we can see in Joseph from this passage. We observe Joseph as the guardian of the family. Joseph took care of his young family as protector and provider. The Bible says, "And the child (Jesus) grew and became strong; He was filled with wisdom, and the grace of God was on Him" (Luke 2:40). In order for Jesus to grow and become strong, His father obviously physically cared for his son. Joseph made a modest living as a carpenter so his wife and son could have the necessities of life. Because Joseph was a good provider, Jesus was filled with wisdom and God's grace was on Him.

I doubt this comes as any surprise to you. However, there is something we must connect. Notice that Joseph made a modest living to give his family what they needed. He had the job; the job did not have him. Joseph never aspired to build an empire around his carpentry skills. He was more interested in building his family in a way that would please the Lord.

Later, Joseph would train Jesus in the carpentry trade. It was the Jewish custom for the father to pass along the family business to his children. Little did Joseph know that he was giving his son the skills He would need to eventually be the primary provider for the family when he was gone. Joseph was a model caregiver for his family.

Mary and Joseph lived out a biblical example of parenting for today's parents to note. Even though there are so few verses describing the early life of Jesus, the Lord has given us a profound look into scriptural parenting. The biblical calling of parents to raise their children in the way they should go can be clearly seen in just these few verses. If the Luke 2 passage is read casually, a much deeper message could easily be missed. We can better understand the weight of Mary and Joseph's calling when seen through the pages of the Old Testament. We are able to appreciate that Joseph was more than just a teacher, worship leader, and caregiver. Joseph was the spiritual leader of the home. Are you up for the challenge?

Home Apps

Tonight, as your children are going to bed, go into each of their rooms and talk about their day. Read a short devotion with them. If you don't have a particular devotion in mind read Genesis 1:1 and Psalms 19:1. You can talk about how God is the creator of all things. The idea behind this home application is for you to start a dialogue with your children. If you are already having this type of conversation with your children, that's great! Then let me suggest a new twist. Instead of leading the devotion time, ask one of your children to lead it.

Day 12

…your Word is truth. (John 17:17b)

Hartford Courant Reporter: "Dr. Graham, do you have any regrets about your family?"
Billy Graham: "I've neglected them. I've traveled too much, written too many articles,
written too many books."

Do you teach your family the Bible?

Jonathan Falwell is the pastor of Thomas Road Baptist Church in Lynchburg, Virginia. He is a busy pastor and a very godly man. In August 2010, he was a guest speaker in a class I was taking at Liberty University. I asked Pastor Falwell if he had devotions with his family. I was not surprised when he said he does nightly devotions with his family. Then Jonathan said,

> *My family loves to come into the master bedroom just before bedtime for devotions. Our four children come in with their Bibles or electronic Bibles in hand. We like to go through books of the Bible during our time. I usually lead in the discussions; however, I often encourage one of my children to lead. This gives them a chance to guide the discussion. We all enjoy this part of the day together.*

Without a doubt, his priority is his family's study of God's Word.

I had another occasion to talk to a very busy and godly pastor and ask him if he and his wife did family devotions. James Merritt, pastor of Cross Pointe Church in Duluth, Georgia, is the father of three boys that are now grown and out of the house. Dr. Merritt said,

> *When my three boys were at home we would do our family devotions at breakfast. We were always together in the mornings. We would learn and memorize a verse of Scripture together and talk about it all throughout the week. When my boys were older, I would occasionally let them take turns leading our morning devotions. Nighttime was special too. Every night I always wanted to pray with them just before they would go to bed. I guess the biggest way I tried to disciple my kids was by living out a Christian example in front of them.*

After reading these two examples, let me ask you a few questions. Did these men ever say anything about pulling out their theology books to lead in their family devotions? Do you think they pointed at their advanced Biblical degrees hanging on the wall and told their children, "Thus saith me?" Or were they making their wife and children sit at attention in the den while standing on the coffee table pounding on their Bibles? No, no, and definitely not. These men were not preaching, lecturing, or even going into deep doctoral dialogue. They could but that is far from necessary.

In the New Testament Paul wrote a letter to his young apprentice, Timothy. He was encouraging him to persevere in his faith and use the gifts the Lord had given him to serve the church. For a moment, Paul reminisces and reminds Timothy how Christ was introduced to him through two very special people. The Bible says, "I am reminded of your sincere faith, which first lived in your grandmother Lois and in your mother Eunice and, I am persuaded, now lives in you also" (2 Tim. 1:5). Scripture has nothing to say regarding Timothy's father, but it is evident that these women shared their faith with him. Grandma and Mom took disciple-making seriously.

These stories have a very special common thread. Each of these people love the Lord, love their families, and want to spend time in the Word with their families. Does this describe you?

Leading in the Word

You can have a significant impact on your children's lives when you spend time as a family in God's Word. But how are you supposed to get started? Where does Scripture stand on this issue? Beginning in the Old Testament, the prophet or prophetess would stand with their backs to God in front of the people on behalf of God and say, "This is what the Lord says." Moses, Miriam, Elijah, Deborah, Jeremiah, Huldah, Isaiah, and Anna were all people who heard the voice of God and declared His Word of truth to the people of God. These men and women were the moral compasses to the nation back then. They were the ones who dictated to the people the ethical values of how they were supposed to live.

In the New Testament the Bible gives another example. Luke describes Mary and Joseph, the earthly parents of Christ, as the primary Bible teachers of Jesus. Luke 2:40 says, "And the child (Jesus) grew and became strong; He was filled with wisdom, and the grace of God was on Him." The fact that Jesus was full of wisdom and God's grace was on Him indicates that Mary and Joseph were obedient to teaching their son God's message of truth. Clearly, the Shema was an integral part of family life. Jim Burns wrote, "The Shema…was likely the first Scripture Jesus learned as a child."[3] Jesus' parents made certain they taught their son biblical truths and principles. Mary and Joseph obviously were students of God's Word and instilled that same hunger for Scripture in their son.

Fathers are seen by the Lord to be the family prophets. Dads are given the responsibility to set the standards in the home. God desires fathers to stand before their families and communicate His message. It is their job to say, "I know the world is saying this…but this is what the Bible says about…" any issue of life. That's why the Bible says, "the father to the children shall make known thy truth" (Isa. 38:19b KJV).

Unfortunately, this is not presently the case. A nationally known author discovered a disturbing trend in families. He observed that men are stepping off the battlefield of being the family prophet and that wives are stepping onto the field in their place. In his book, *Raising Godly Children in an Ungodly World*, Ken Ham discussed the role reversal that is occurring today. He said,

> In too many cases, neither the mother nor the father is fulfilling the responsibility to train their children in the things of God. In the homes where some training is happening, the mother is usually the one that teaches, prays, and reads the Scriptures without her husband's help… Mothers seem to be taking on the leadership roles more and more; fathers are opting out of this area all together… In the majority of Christian homes, it is usually the mother, not the father, who acts as the spiritual head.[4]

Taken a step further, a local survey was conducted in which several questions were asked of Christian fathers and mothers. The investigation found an even more troubling development. One of the questions asked in the study was, "Who typically leads the family devotion time?" An astonishing 45% of the parents polled answered, "We don't do family devotion time."[5] This is dangerous ground for families to be treading. If parents do not take ownership of biblical training in the home, there is little chance their children will be a growing Bible student when they get out of the house and are living on their own. Christian Smith wrote, "Most teenagers and their parents may not realize it, but a lot of research in the sociology of religion suggests that the most important social influence in shaping young people's religious lives is the religious life modeled and taught to them by their parents."[6] Where do you think families are heading? Where is your family heading? It has been estimated that by the time the millennial generation (those born between the years 1982 -2000) reaches adulthood, only 5% will be Bible believers and going to church.[7] Can parents, especially dads, afford to neglect being the prophet of the family any longer?

Is it time to stop the cycle? Dads can reclaim their God-given responsibility. It is never too late. God is not expecting perfection but persistence. He desires all believers to read and study His Word and strive to maintain a life that honors Him. Are you involved in a Bible study group with other believers? Do you have someone in your life holding you accountable in your journey with the Lord? When parents, especially dads, run after God in this way, they will be able to lead and teach their family well.

Sam is a husband and dad of four children. He and his wife Linda have two biological sons and two adopted daughters. They are great parents who love their kids. Sam's a high school and technical college graduate. He used to own his own electrical contractor business but now works for a local company as an electrician. Linda is a college graduate and works as a computer programmer. They are the picture of the all-American family except for one thing. About two years ago, Sam and Linda made a choice that many Christian families consider but never follow through with. He decided to set aside Sunday nights for family devotions. Recently, I asked Sam about their devotion time and this is what he said,

> *Family devotions are a great experience each week. As the head of the family, I feel it is my job to lead our devotion time together. It is very humbling. I love the closeness we share together around the Word of God. It's been a great learning time for my family but I think I get more out of it than they do. It's almost indescribable. When it comes down to it, more than anything, I want my children to see their earthly father humbled before the heavenly Father. I wouldn't take anything for our family devotion time.*

I love Sam's heart. Sam is a great example of a father leading his wife and children as the family prophet. It just goes to show you when fathers take their responsibility as the family prophet seriously God can do extraordinary things.

What do you do when you have less than the ideal marital situation? For guidance we need to look no further than 1 Samuel. Hannah was a godly woman who desired to have a child, but for some reason the Lord had chosen not to allow her to get pregnant. This was only one of Hannah's problems. Her other problem was that she had a marriage that was not the greatest. She was married to Elkanah who loved her very much. However, Elkanah also had another wife named Peninnah. Even though Elkanah loved Hannah more, Peninnah was able to have children. This situation created a great deal of tension in the family. Nonetheless, Hannah was determined. She earnestly prayed to the Lord and begged Him to give her a son. In return, Hannah promised to give him back to serve the Lord for the rest of his life. Even though we are never in a position to negotiate with God, He took her up on her offer and gave her a son. During the first three years of his life Hannah loved, cared, and taught her baby in order to prepare him for service to the Lord. She was the perfect example of a godly mother.

Mom, perhaps you find yourself in a less than ideal marriage situation. Hannah teaches us three very important truths. First, love the Lord. Hannah knew if she was ever going to have children she had to go to the Lord who was the giver of all things. In her prayer we see how she viewed God. She said, "Oh Lord" (1 Sam. 1:11) which is translated Jehovah, meaning 'the supreme God.' Hannah acknowledged that in her prayer. Second, even though her home situation was not the best, she loved her husband. It's clear that Hannah and Peninnah's relationship was not the greatest, but there is absolutely no hint of any problems between Hannah and Elkanah. In 1 Samuel 1:8 we see a tender moment between the two that shows his concern for his wife and her love for her husband. Third, she loved her son. Hannah modeled the verse that Solomon would later write in Proverbs 22:6. She trained her son in the way he should go so he could serve the Lord just as she had promised.

It all comes down to this. Children need someone in their lives leading them scripturally. No matter if you're a single parent who has to be the leader of the home, the only parent in the home motivated to lead, or a couple working together as a team, you all have the same responsibility. Your task is to lead your children to the throne of Grace and into the presence of the Lord through His infallible Word.

Home Apps

At bedtime tonight or at breakfast in the morning, set aside some time to discuss a verse of Scripture. Read Isaiah 40:8 and ask each member of the family to describe what they think God is saying. The goal of this time is to get your family reading and talking about God's Word. When these types of conversations begin, the Holy Spirit can do incredible things.

Day 13

After I looked things over, I stood up and said to the nobles, the officials and the rest of the people, "Don't be afraid of them. Remember the Lord, who is great and awesome, and fight for your families, your sons and your daughters, your wives and your homes." (Neh. 4:14)

"You can do more than pray after you have prayed, but you cannot do more than pray until you have prayed."
— John Bunyan author of Pilgrim's Progress

Are you praying for your children?

On October 4, 1997, God showed me the unbelievable power of prayer. It was a day I'll never forget. It was a beautiful fall Saturday in Washington D.C on the National Mall. I was attending the Promise Keepers event called Stand in the Gap. Men from all over the country came to one location to worship the Lord. Some have estimated that over one million men came to our nation's capital to pray. The day was filled with prayer and praise of the Almighty God. But there was one moment in particular that still stands out to me to this day. At one point during the event the speaker asked the men to pull out of their wallets pictures of the people closest to them. I didn't have any pictures of my family with me, but I remember putting my face on the ground and visualizing the faces of my gorgeous wife, my beautiful daughter, and my handsome son. Their faces were as if they were standing right in front of me. As I was being led to pray, it was as if I was praying for the first time. I prayed for my wife's spiritual maturity, the purity of her heart and mind, and her ability to grow as a wife and a mother. For my children I prayed for their salvation, spiritual growth, future mates, wisdom, and everything in between. I had always prayed for my family before…at least I thought I had. I may have missed a few days here and there but I would pray…most of the time. I would ask God to be with my family, bless my children, and then move on to the next topic. I thought that was enough.

The fact of the matter was that was not enough, and I knew I needed to do better. I wanted to pray more but just never made it a big priority. However, that day changed my thinking. It was a pivotal moment for me. With my face on the ground, I realized how flippant I had been in my prayer time for these three precious people. God let me see how sporadic my prayer time was and how superficial my prayers were for the three people I love so much. The Lord let me see I needed to change. He showed me that I needed to pray specifically for them, stand in the gap in intercession, and consistently pray for my family. From that moment on I have made praying for my wife and my children a major priority in my prayer life. How about your prayer time? Is it inconsistent or generalized when you pray?

Leading in Prayer

As we discovered in Day 12's reading, children need prophets and/or prophetesses in their families. God has given parents the awesome privilege and responsibility to stand with their backs to Him in front of their families on His behalf and say, "This is what the Lord says." But God has another important task for you as well. Children need to have a family priest. In the Old Testament, the priest turned his back to the people, looked toward God and interceded on behalf of the people. The priests were the mediators, the bridge between God and man. They also led the people of God into the presence of the Lord. People like Melchizedek, Aaron, Hannah, Eli, Mary, and Anna all sought after God for others. These people stood in the gap before God for the people of God.

Let's look back into the home of Jesus and see how Mary and Joseph modeled this for us. The Bible says in Luke 2:41, "Every year His parents went to Jerusalem for the Feast of the Passover."

It is evident that Mary and Joseph were dedicated to obeying God's requirements for all Jewish customs and celebrations. Luke goes on to say, "When He was twelve years old, they went up to the Feast, according to the custom" (Lk. 2:42). According to these verses, Jesus and His family annually attended the Passover. Kent Hughes, in his commentary of Luke, described what Jesus would have experienced during the Passover celebration. Hughes said,

> At about 3:00PM the sacrifice began. We may well surmise that Joseph and his relatives, in preparation for Jesus' manhood, took preadolescent Jesus into the temple with them so He could observe the sacrifice. If so, as the gates of the temple court closed behind the vast group of worshipers, He heard a ram's horn sound and saw Joseph, in concert with hundreds of other worshipers, slaughter his family's lamb. The priests, standing in two long rows, caught the blood in gold and silver basins, then doused it against the base of the altar. Levites sang the Hallel Psalms (113 – 118) above the din as Jesus' father dressed his lamb and, before leaving, slung the animal, wrapped in its own skin, over his shoulder and departed with his young son in tow.[8]

Every year at the Passover celebration, Joseph was the family priest.

Even today the Lord sees parents as the family priests. God expects you to stand and face Him on behalf of your family. It is your responsibility to come before the Lord to intercede for your family. James Merritt, author of *In a World of...Friends, Foes, and Fools*, said, "I am convinced you can do nothing greater for your kids (and future generations) than to pray for them continuously."[9] There is no greater work. Parents are given a great honor and privilege to bridge the gap and lift up their families to the Heavenly Father.

In a study conducted for this book, several questions were asked of Christian men regarding their prayer life. One of the questions asked was "During an average week, how many days do you specifically pray for your child(ren)?" 67% of the men polled said they pray 5-7 times per week for their children. Only 5% said they never pray for their children.[10] When I was at Promise Keepers I would have fallen into the 67% group too. Women were also asked the same question. 70% of the women said they pray 5-7 times per week for their children with only 4% saying they never pray for their children.[11] These results are somewhat encouraging; however, my question is what are you specifically praying for?

Patrick Morley, in his book *The Man in the Mirror*, gave this list as an offering to fathers to use as a guide in their prayer time for their children. He listed:

- *A saving faith (thanksgiving if already Christian),*
- *A growing faith,*
- *An independent faith (as they get older),*
- *To be strong and healthy in mind, body, and spirit,*

- *A sense of destiny (purpose),*
- *A desire for integrity,*
- *A call to excellence,*
- *To understand the ministry God has for them,*
- *That I will set aside times to spend with them,*
- *To acquire wisdom,*
- *Protection against drugs, alcohol, and premarital sex,*
- *The mate God has for them (alive somewhere, needing prayer),*
- *Glorify the Lord in everything.[12]*

Children that live in this world today are constantly bombarded with these issues. Is there a better source of power than prayer? Let me ask, if your kid's survival depended on your prayers how would they be doing?

The Bible says in 1 Peter 5:8b, "Your enemy the devil prowls around like a roaring lion looking for someone to devour." This statement could not be more true, especially for teens in this day and time. God has given you a crucial task. It is time for you to step up and fight for your children, especially if your children are teenagers. Satan has you and your children in his crosshairs. Your whole family is being preyed upon. So let me ask, are they being prayed for?

I talk to people all the time about their prayer time. The number one reason I hear most concerning a Christian's prayer life is "not making the time to pray." To that I suggest making an appointment with God. Remember the elephant? Set a time and keep it…just like reading your Bible. Start with one minute a day. You can increase the time as you go but don't miss your scheduled meeting. However, the second reason people tell me they do not have a consistent prayer life is they feel God is not hearing them. There is not a Christian on the planet who has not felt that way. Every believer at one time or another has felt like his or her prayers were going nowhere and not being heard.

On December 7, 1988, an earthquake registering 6.9 in magnitude shook the city of Spitak, Armenia. In the quake hundreds of buildings were flattened leaving thousands of people trapped in the rubble. During the first few hours, emergency workers were able to rescue many people buried by the debris. Unfortunately, rescuers began losing hope of finding people alive as each day passed. However, one loving father refused to quit. This dad went to the collapsed structure where his son's school once stood. Working tirelessly at the ruins of the school where his son was buried by the quake, he moved bricks, lumber, and other debris with his bare hands, working all day and all night. It was as if he was superhuman. Two days turned into three. Three days turned into four. Four turned into five. The father was exhausted. People were encouraging him to just give up. All hope seemed lost. Then on the sixth day after the earthquake, he removed a section of debris and was able to hear several voices faintly calling out for help. With newfound energy he dug harder than before. He called out his son's name and quietly listened. To his amazement, he heard his son's voice say, "Daddy…I thought you had given up!"

It's easy to feel like that little boy and get weary when we pray. Sometimes we feel that God is not hearing and has given up on us. That's not true. That's never the case. The Bible says, "For the eyes of the Lord are on the righteous and His ears are attentive to their prayer" (1 Pet. 3:12). God says, "I'm listening." God always hears. God always listens. I think where our confusion comes from is that we expect God to answer "yes" to all our prayers or we expect Him to give us an answer immediately. God does answer. Sometimes it's a "yes," sometimes it's a "no," then other times He says, "wait." However, there is another factor to understand. The Bible says, "It's your sins that have cut you off from God. Because of your sins, He has turned away and will not listen anymore" (Isa. 59:2 NLT). We have to be determined to say, "I will ask God to forgive me of my sins. I will make praying for my family the highest priority of my prayer life. No matter what I'm feeling, I know God is listening."

Let me ask you a painful question. If you do not pray for your children, who will? Parents must be the ones who pray for their children. You need to determine to be the priest of the family, make an appointment with the Lord, and "pray continually" (1 Thess. 5:17). So let me ask, is it worth the effort? If you're not praying for them, you can rest assured they are being preyed upon every moment of every day.

Home Apps

Today go before the Lord and sincerely ask God to forgive you of your sins. Ask Him to bring back to your memory the sins you've committed (Psalms 139:23-24) and specifically ask Him to forgive you. Next, take the list above and pray! Pray like you've never prayed before. Ask a friend to pray with you for your children. Invite your spouse, a parent, another relative, or a best friend. No matter who you ask, pray! God works when we pray.

Day 14

"For my thoughts are not your thoughts, neither are your ways my ways," declares the Lord. (Isa. 55:8)

"Never be afraid to trust an unknown future to a known God."
Corrie Ten Boom.

How do you define priority?

A lighthouse operator was given enough oil for one month. His task was to simply keep the light burning every night for the ships passing by the rugged coastline. One day a nearby neighbor came to the operator and asked for some oil to keep his lamps burning. It was a simple request, so the operator helped out his neighbor. A few days later, an old friend from across town asked if he could have some oil to keep his family warm. The keeper sympathized with his friend and gave him some oil. The man assured the operator he would pay him back as soon as he could. He was glad to help out his friends and didn't give it a second thought.

Unfortunately, by the end of the month, the tank in the lighthouse ran dry. That particular night the lighthouse lamp went out and the coastline went dark. Three ships crashed on the rocks and more than one hundred people lost their lives. A government official investigated the incident. The lighthouse operator explained what he had done for his friends and why. The official said, "You were given one task and one task alone. Your job was to keep the lighthouse light burning. Nothing else mattered."

Look at this story with your children in mind and consider this one question about discipleship. What could possibly be more important in the lives of your children than helping them grow spiritually? I hope by now you're saying 'nothing!' God has blessed you with children and the chance to be their spiritual leader. You know in order to make discipleship a reality in your home, something has to happen, but you're not sure what. We've covered some important subjects such as personal discipleship, spending time with your family in the Word, and setting aside time to pray for your family. But piecing them together can be at best challenging if not overwhelming. The answer is simple but the work behind it may be difficult. The answer is this: make your family a priority. It is a simple idea that requires dedication and a reorganization of many, if not all, aspects of your life. I know some reading this book have done well at making family a priority. On the other hand, there are those who have not. Whatever category you find yourself in, we all need help and encouragement to stay on track. That's why God has given us some priceless insights through several women and men in the Bible who made their families a priority. Two people in particular lived their lives by simple, straightforward philosophies, setting an example for us today of how to make our family a priority.

Family as a Priority – A Woman's Perspective

Without a doubt, one of the first people we need to get our training from is a woman from the Old Testament. This lady is not someone you hear much about, but you've probably heard of her kids. She was the mother of Moses, Aaron, and Miriam, and one of the great, unsung heroes of the Bible. Jochebed and her family were slaves in Egypt during a time when God was physically adding to many homes. In a very dark time for the Hebrew nation the Lord was allowing families to have babies left and right. The population increase made the Pharaoh nervous so he decided to implement some birth control. He decreed that every Hebrew midwife must murder any Hebrew boy that was born. Fortunately, the midwives feared God more than Pharaoh and allowed the boys to live. Since his first plan didn't work, Pharaoh commanded the Egyptian people to carry out this massacre. He ordered his people to throw any Hebrew boy two years old or younger into the Nile River. As you can imagine, times were hard and stressful, but God was in control. Through God's sovereign hand, Moses, the future leader of the Hebrew people, was born. Under the circumstances Jochebed had to take special care to keep Moses hidden for three months. She displayed great faith in the Lord, knowing He would protect her child. As Moses grew older, hiding him became more difficult, and she knew her time was running out. Jochebed put her faith into action as she wisely conceived a brilliant plan. She built the first unsinkable floating baby carriage and placed it, with baby inside, along the banks in the Nile River. In our minds we can't fathom making such a daring move. How could a mother expose her child to such danger? A floating basket…a baby alone in the water…what was she thinking? As bad as all that sounds, that was not the worst part. The Nile River is home to one of the most ferocious animals on earth, the Nile crocodile. This bit of information now makes Jochebed a candidate for a mental institution. But before we commit her too quickly, we need to take one thing into consideration. Not only did she put her faith into action, but she also trusted in God's sovereignty. Perhaps the Lord gave her a glimpse into the future of her baby; the Bible doesn't say. But one thing we do know: Jochebed gave strict instructions for Miriam to stay close to the miniature ark to see what the Lord would do. In typical God-like fashion, the unbelievable happened. God allowed the boat to be found by none other than the Pharaoh's daughter. She was possibly the only person in Egypt who could sway the thinking of her father to keep this baby alive. She had the unidentified craft brought to her by her servant, looked inside, and found something that would eventually change the lives of millions of people. She found baby Moses crying, right on cue I might add, inside the basket and he captured the princess's heart. Just a short distance away, as Jochebed had directed, Miriam was waiting for her chance to act. As she watched everything unfold, Miriam decided to make her move and offer the new mother some childcare assistance.

When we consider this episode from the Bible, Jochebed gives us some invaluable insights into the principles by which she lived. First, we see a woman whose ultimate priority was to love and trust the Lord in spite of the fact that her situation was going from bad to worse. Jochebed had no power to do anything about Pharaoh's edict, yet she put her faith completely in God. She knew that the Lord was ultimately the one in control, not Pharaoh. Sometimes we find ourselves in out-of-control, difficult, and stressful situations. Guess who allowed you to be put there? God did. Guess who wants to walk with and guide you every step of the way? Of course God does. Jochebed teaches us to love and trust the Lord completely.

Second, our heroin illustrates how to put our faith into action. Jochebed was at the end of her rope, so she courageously put her baby in a waterproof basket. Even though she did not have a plan, she knew God did. She did everything she could do and then trusted the Lord to do the miraculous. God used her simple act of faith and the nation's dilemma to place Moses in the hands of the only person on the planet who could protect him. Pharaoh's daughter was the key component in God's overall plan to begin the process of preparing a leader for the Hebrew people. He used it to train His future leader, free His people, and eventually lead them to the Promised Land. Is it any different with you and your children? God has it all in His more than capable hands. Are you doing the little things the Lord wants you to do and trusting Him with the big things?

Lastly, consider how influential Jochebed's children became to the Hebrew people. Moses became the leader and lawgiver to the people. Aaron became the spokesman for Moses and the priest to the nation. Miriam became one of Israel's prohetesses. How did they become such great leaders? You don't have to look any further than the mother who made her family a priority. Through the passages of the Old Testament we see Jochebed's influence lived out in the lives of each of her three children. Although they were not perfect, Moses, Aaron, and Miriam loved God and put their faith into action, just like mom.

Family as a Priority – A Man's Perspective

Another example of making family a priority is found in two very ordinary and unsuspecting people. Mary and Joseph were given the privilege to be the earthly parents of Jesus. We don't have much information about this young couple; nevertheless, the Bible gives us some insight into how they were able to make family their priority. What was their secret? While we're on the subject, what was so special about them, in particular Joseph, that God would give him the responsibility to be the earthly father of the Savior of the world? What principles did he live by that made him different? As expected, the Bible has the answers. Matthew records,

> This is how the birth of Jesus the Messiah came about: His mother Mary was pledged to be married to Joseph, but before they came together, she was found to be pregnant through the Holy Spirit. Because Joseph her husband was faithful to the law, and yet did not want to expose her to public disgrace, he had in mind to divorce her quietly. But after he had considered this, an angel of the Lord appeared to him in a dream and said, "Joseph son of David, do not be afraid to take Mary home as your wife, because what is conceived in her is from the Holy Spirit. She will give birth to a son, and you are to give Him the name Jesus, because He will save His people from their sins." All this took place to fulfill what the Lord had said through the prophet: "The virgin will conceive and give birth to a son, and they will call Him Immanuel" (which means "God with us"). When Joseph woke up, he did what the angel of the Lord had commanded him and took Mary home as his wife. (Mt. 1:18-24)

As we see in this passage, Joseph was a simple man who lived by simple principles. He was a man who based his decisions on God's Word, put others first, and acted on what he believed. Joseph utilized these qualities as he made his family a priority.

The first principle we see in Joseph's life is that he lived by God's standards. The Bible refers to him as a "husband faithful to the law" (Mt. 1:19a). When Joseph found out Mary was pregnant, he knew he had to do something. It was reasonable for him to think that Mary had been with another man. He felt he could not go through with the marriage because he was not the father of the baby. This would violate his moral standards. Joseph had every right to divorce Mary. In this situation we see a man who stood firmly on God's Word. He was a student of the Bible and was determined to live his life according to God's standard. Joseph was a man who made his decisions based on the Word of God, no matter what the situation.

Putting others first is the second principle we see in Joseph's life. He was justified to divorce Mary; the only question was how would he carry it out? Because of his love and kindness toward her, he did not want to put her through "public disgrace" let alone have her put to death (Deut. 22:23-24). Instead he decided on another alternative. The Bible says Joseph "had in mind to divorce her quietly" (Mt. 1:19b). In this we see that Joseph was more concerned for Mary's reputation. He had every right to expose her sin publicly and humiliate her in front of the whole town. However, his concern was not for himself. He decided to make the divorce a private matter with only two other people as witnesses. He did this because he wanted to protect his former 'wife to be' as long as he could. In these verses we see a man who put Mary first. Joseph was a man who put others before himself, no matter the situation.

The third principle we see in Joseph's life was that he was a man of action. When Joseph woke up from his dream the Bible says, "he did what the angel of the Lord had commanded him" (Mt. 1:24). Joseph was faced with an embarrassing situation. Nevertheless, he lived by God's laws and made them the standard by which he lived. When God gave him a new assignment through a dream, hesitation was not in Joseph's character as he acted on God's command. He wanted to live a righteous life before God no matter what it cost. I can imagine he felt liberated by the angel's announcement. Joseph was a doer of God's Word.

Although this is far from an exhaustive list, these are three key factors in making family a priority from a man's perspective. Do you ever consider God's Word when you are making decisions, large or small? Do you put other people before yourself or before your golf game? How about what your family sees in you on a daily basis? Are you striving to make your thoughts, words, and actions match what would please the Lord? Make your family a priority, as did Joseph, and allow God to do the miraculous.

Getting Personal

Parents are given the responsibility to provide for their families the things they need to prosper and flourish. This provision does not necessarily mean earthly wealth, but it does mean basic necessities. These basic necessities include a positive and stable home environment, physical health, food, and shelter. It is the parent's job to make sure these needs are met so that children can have the chance to thrive. But here's the thing: believers and non-believers alike can provide for the physical needs of their children. But God expects more from His followers. Godly parents are called to make the home a place where their children can be "filled with wisdom, and the grace of God" (Lk. 2:40b) will be on them. That means we need to learn from people like Jochebed and Joseph and the principles they lived by. The Lord has given us their examples so we too can learn their secret of making family a priority.

You may have the idea that too much time has gone by and you are too old and set in your ways to make any changes. That's not true. You may be thinking, "I know I need to step up and make my family a priority, but if I try to make any sudden modifications now I'll just be seen as the court jester and not taken seriously." It may be difficult at first, but you have to be willing to take the chance.

Regardless of what has happened in the past, you have to understand and believe there is always hope. It is never too late to learn and implement new principles. It is never too late to make changes in your life and adjustments in your priorities. Sparky Anderson, long-time manager of the Cincinnati Reds, once said, "People who live in the past generally are afraid to compete in the present. I've got my faults, but living in the past is not one of them. There's no future in it."[13] It's never too late, especially when God is involved. You may need to go slowly at first, but in time, you will make a difference. However, there is one catch. You have to be willing to make the transition to God's ways, not your own ways. You have to be willing to live by these principles at all costs. It has to start with you. Is it God's will and purpose that you make your family a priority? Yes! Let me ask, 'Is your family worth the effort?' If so, put yourself and your family in God's hands and believe along with Job, "I know that you can do all things; no purpose of yours can be thwarted" (Job 42:2). By the way, the reason God trusted Joseph to be the earthy father of the Savior of the world is the same reason He has given you the children in your home. He loves and believes in you.

Home Apps

Tonight or tomorrow night at dinner make it a point to have the entire family sit together at the kitchen or dining room table. Just as everyone sits down, ask an open-ended question to see how each person responds. The question is, "What was one thing that made you laugh today?" If your family is not accustomed to this type of dinner introduction then maybe you need to give the first answer. The goal is to get your family talking about something humorous and light. Then let the conversation go wherever the Lord takes it.

Day 15

"Meaningless! Meaningless!" says the Teacher. "Utterly meaningless! Everything is meaningless." (Ecc. 1:2)

"Whenever you find yourself on the side of the majority, it is time to pause and reflect."
— Mark Twain

Are you having true success?

In a small coastal town of Louisiana, a successful businessman was getting his 22-foot sailboat ready to launch out for a day of recreation in the Gulf of Mexico. The sun was just coming up on a beautiful Friday morning, and the weather forecast had predicted a perfect day to be on the water. As the businessman was making final preparations, a shrimp boat pulled into the slip next to him. He couldn't help noticing the large number of shrimp the boat was bringing in. Intrigued, the man asked the fisherman, "How long did it take you to catch all those shrimp?" The fisherman replied, "Not very long, I was only out about three hours." The man said, "Three hours. Why didn't you stay out longer and catch more shrimp?" The fisherman said, "This is enough for today. What I'll get paid for this catch will take care of me and my family's needs." The man said, "It's still early. What will you do with the rest of your day?" The fisherman laughed and said, "I'll go home; eat breakfast with my wife and children; get the kids ready and take them to school; come back home and help my wife with some things around the house. My wife and I will go into town and eat lunch together and do a little shopping. After that, it will be about time for the kids to get home from school. I'll help them with their homework, go outside and play with them, and before you know it, it will be dinnertime. We'll eat together, clean up the dishes, and watch TV. Then it will be time for bed." The man could not believe what he was hearing. He said, "You cannot be serious. You can do much better than that. I have a MBA from Harvard and I can help you." "What do you have in mind?" asked the fisherman. "Well, first of all you need to spend more time fishing. By increasing your hours you'll make extra money. With the extra money you could buy a bigger boat. Given time, you could buy more boats until you have a fleet of shrimp boats. With the increased volume, you could sell your catch to the fish processing plant yourself instead of a middleman. Over time you could open your own processing plant. You could catch the shrimp, process the shrimp, and distribute the shrimp all on your own. You could leave this little Louisiana town and move to New York where you could expand and build your enterprise." The fisherman was impressed and asked, "This sounds interesting. How long do you think this would take?" The businessman said, "If you work hard it could take twenty maybe twenty-five years." "Then what?" asked the fisherman. The man with a gleam in his eye replied, "Once you've built your empire you could sell the company and make millions." "Then what?" the fisherman asked again. "Then you could retire, move back here with your family, and enjoy life." The shrimp boat fisherman thought for several minutes and said, "twenty to twenty-five years is a long time. My kids would be grown and out on their own by then. I would miss so much time with them and my wife. Why would I want to do all that?" Then he paused and said, "No thanks! I have everything I need right now."

The shrimp boat fisherman and the Harvard businessman had two different approaches on life, time, and family. From the businessman's perspective, making money was priority, but from the fisherman's standpoint, family came first. Many parents struggle with juggling work pressures and home responsibilities. Let's stop and imagine life from the fisherman's perspective. Visualize yourself thirty to forty years from now. Your children are grown and have families of their own. You are finally getting to enjoy spoiling grandchildren. What kind of life do you want to see your kids and grandkids living? I'm not talking about careers, finances, social obligations, or the size of their house. That's small stuff. I'm talking about things that matter, things like their spiritual health. Do they love the Lord with all their hearts, souls, minds, and strength? Are they transferring that love of the Lord to their children? What about their careers? Of course, you want to see them be good providers. Having good jobs to support their families is necessary. But the real question isn't do they have a job…rather does their job have them? Workaholism is real. How about balance? Do they have margin in their lives? Do they run from event to practice to game to meeting to obligation to the store…you get the point? Days like those are enough to make your head spin. Who wants a steady diet of busyness? Having margin is the exact opposite of busyness. Would you like to see them with room in their day, in their week to have down time, family time, and time with God? Do they have time to love God in every aspect of their lives? Margin means going to bed at night and waking up ready for a new day. Mayhem, on the other hand, means collapsing in bed at night only to wake up back in the rat race again. Which sounds more appealing? Now let's come back to the present. There are major advantages in living a life loving the Lord, making family a priority, and having margin. Before you think it, I'm not anti-making money, anti-career, or anti-success. However, I do think that people can focus too much on these areas. So let me ask, if some part of the fisherman's lifestyle seems attractive to you, what do you need to do today to make that kind of lifestyle a reality for everybody's future?

God's heart is to have the children in every home growing spiritually, being led in God's Word daily, being prayed for constantly, and living in an environment where family is a priority. But so many people fall prey to three common pitfalls that distract from their focus. They are:

- *Deception # 1 – To succeed means to have a dynamic career*
- *Deception # 2 – I am doing this for my family*
- *Deception # 3 – Money will solve my problems*[14]

These are three of a long list of common deceptions that preoccupy many people. However, a parent who is running after God can overcome each of these myths and become the spiritual leader his family needs. Confronting these deceptions will give your children the best chance to be filled with wisdom and have God's grace abound in their lives.

Deception # 1 – To succeed means to have a dynamic career

Deception # 1 has taken many parents captive in today's culture. People feel that if they want to be successful they have to be the best at what they do. This mentality has many consequences that will drain a parent's most valuable resource – time. Too many men and women think success revolves around their careers, climbing the corporate ladder, but the Bible sees it another way. The truth of the matter is, "Work alone cannot produce a success that matters."[15]

No one knew this truth better than the wisest man to ever live: King Solomon. There was nothing he did not achieve. In Ecclesiastes 2:4-11 the Bible says,

> I undertook great projects: I built houses for myself and planted vineyards. I made gardens and parks and planted all kinds of fruit trees in them. I made reservoirs to water groves of flourishing trees. I bought male and female slaves and had other slaves who were born in my house. I also owned more herds and flocks than anyone in Jerusalem before me. I amassed silver and gold for myself, and the treasure of kings and provinces. I acquired male and female singers, and a harem as well—the delights of a man's heart. I became greater by far than anyone in Jerusalem before me. In all this my wisdom stayed with me. I denied myself nothing my eyes desired; I refused my heart no pleasure. My heart took delight in all my labor, and this was the reward for all my toil. Yet when I surveyed all that my hands had done and what I had toiled to achieve, everything was meaningless, a chasing after the wind; nothing was gained under the sun.

Solomon jolts his reader after a long list of what seems to represent success by saying, "everything was meaningless, a chasing after the wind" (Ecc. 2:11b). The reality of this passage is that no amount of achievement can possibly attain fulfillment. Of course, you need a job and giving your employer your best is the Biblical thing to do. However, you do the math. All the extra time you give to your job reduces and robs what you could give to your family. It is possible to overcome this deception by making your family a priority, not your career. How do you define success? God defines success as a parent leading his or her family spiritually.

Deception # 2 – I am doing this for my family

Deception # 2 is another fallacy that has taken many people captive in today's culture. Some men and women feel that in order to justify Deception # 1, they must use Deception # 2 as an excuse. The reality of the issue is you're not doing it for your family; you're doing it for yourself. You want to look good to your boss, you want the promotion, or you want to get to the next step on the ladder. Again I'm not saying that these pursuits are wrong. However, when these pursuits constantly take you away from home and out of the lives of the people God has entrusted you with, there is a problem. "What our families really want is more of us."[16] To put it simply, they need more of the best of their parents. However, the reality of life is that when you get home from a busy day, there are times you have little to give. Rod Cooper stated, "The number one issue I see in counseling teens is that 90% are suffering with depression. The reason they are depressed is because they have no one to connect to."[17] To put it simply, you are the one that they connect to best. On the other hand, having significant others in their lives is important too. I cannot emphasize this point enough; however, you are by far their greatest asset.

You can overcome this deception by not hiding behind this excuse. If this is an issue in your life, don't waste another minute. Get back in your home and be mentally present and physically engaged. It takes balance. Again, in your mind, define success. God defines success as a parent who spends quality time with his family and strives to lead them spiritually.

Deception # 3 – Money will solve my problems

Deception # 3 is another erroneous belief that has taken many people hostage in today's culture. Without question, families have to have money; however, families have to avoid letting money have them. When parents allow money to control their thinking, many problems can arise. The biggest problem that surfaces, according to Rod Cooper, is the "Creeping Decimal-ism"[18] mindset. Cooper said, "Creeping decimal-ism means I have $10, then I want $100, next I have $100, then I want $1,000 and so on."[19] In reality, more money only creates more problems than they can possibly solve. King Solomon again provides wisdom in this area. The Bible says in Ecclesiastes 5:10-12, "Whoever loves money never has enough; whoever loves wealth is never satisfied with their income. This too is meaningless. As goods increase, so do those who consume them. And what benefit are they to the owners except to feast their eyes on them? The sleep of a laborer is sweet, whether they eat little or much, but as for the rich, their abundance permits them no sleep." The bottom line is that success is not defined by a career or money. No amount of money can possibly compensate for failure at home. Money is to be used for provision and ministry, not to be stockpiled. Men and women can overcome this deception by seeing money as a tool that ultimately belongs to God. Families need parents to pursue being spiritual leaders not running after monetary gain. These deceptions are powerful forces. What will it take for you to finally say "no" to these deceptions and say "yes" to being at home more and raising your children?

Bobby Bowden, the longtime football coach of Florida State University, has seen the effect of parents setting a poor example firsthand. In a message he delivered at a Fellowship of Christian Athletes event, he told a story of a time he was asked about the change he has seen in the players he recruited and coached. The question was, "Have the boys you've coached changed over the years?"[20] Astonishingly he said, "No, they haven't changed."[21] He went on to say, "The people who have changed are the parents."[22] He then clarified his statement by saying, "The parents have quit raising their kids."[23]

Making the Connection

After Moses was taken into heaven, God placed Joshua in charge of leading the Hebrew nation into the Promised Land. Joshua was not afraid to take on new challenges, never saw anything too big for God, and wanted to give his life in service to the Lord. As God's appointed man, Joshua called together the leaders of Israel to remind them of the Lord's faithfulness and goodness and challenged them to make a choice about their allegiance. Then he said, "As for me and my house, we will serve the Lord" (Josh. 24:15b). Notice how he words his statement. He was direct and to the point. His proclamation wasn't only about himself but everyone who lived at his address. They all were going to be God's servants. But don't think for a minute that he was the only one in his house who loved the Lord and everyone else was forced. No way! His entire family loved and wanted to serve God because they first saw it lived out in their father. He was the spiritual leader of his home and he was encouraging the leaders of Israel to do the same. How about you? Are you the spiritual leader of your home? If you are a single parent, then the Lord has called you to be the spiritual leader of your home. Maybe you're the only parent who is interested in discipling your children. Then the Lord has called you to be the spiritual leader of your home. If you have a spouse, then together give your children what they so desperately need. No matter what the case, your children need spiritual leadership.

Home Apps

Before you go to bed tonight set aside some time to pray. Find someone who is close to you. If you're single, ask your best friend or one of your parents. If you're married this is an exercise to do with your spouse. Keep in mind this needs to be someone who loves you and your family. Ask this person to pray with you specifically about your children's spiritual growth and future. This can be done over the phone, Skype, or in person. No matter who your prayer partner is, this one act has the potential to make radical differences in the future of your children. In addition, it can bring you closer to your prayer partner.

A DIFFERENT APPROACH

Read This First – Week 4 Intro…

The old saying, "Everything rises and falls on leadership" is very true. The tremendous task the Lord has given parents to lead their families can seem overwhelming. That's why it is so important for parents to base their leadership style on biblical principles, which makes this week's reading so essential.

Our journey this week will give us a chance to explore a deeper meaning behind the second part of Proverbs 22:6. This is the part of the verse that says, "in the way your child should go." We will be taking an in-depth look at this phrase which will lead us to make some new discoveries. One of the biggest discoveries we will make is our need to be more informed and discerning about the culture in which our children live. In addition, we will see the need to actually be students of our own children.

As we continue our reading this week, we will be encouraged to investigate the subject of our children's style of learning. Knowing your child's learning style has the potential to unlock a new world of opportunities that can help you in your discipleship efforts. From there, our challenge will be to utilize the DG^2 strategy which can help us direct our children in the way they should go.

Do not forsake wisdom, and she will protect you; love her, and she will watch over you. The beginning of wisdom is this: Get wisdom. Though it cost all you have, get understanding. Cherish her, and she will exalt you; embrace her, and she will honor you. (Prov. 4:6-8)

"When all else fails read the directions."
— Al Smith

Day 16

A good person who gives in to a bad person is a muddied spring, a polluted well. (Prov. 25:26)

James Merritt was asked, "What would you consider to be the top three things attacking the family?" He quickly responded, "Materialism, media, and morality."[1]

Do you study your children?

Years ago in seminary during an evangelism class our professor showed a video called EE-Taow! The Mouk People. The Mouk tribe lives in Papua New Guinea. They were very superstitious, believed in ancestry reincarnation, and lived in a great deal of fear. God called Mark and Gloria Zook as missionaries to this group of people. The video showed a reenactment of the tribe's salvation experience. It was very moving and powerful.

Watching the video I was riveted to the Zook's story, their sacrifice, and how they shared the Gospel. The missionaries took about two years to study the Mouk language and their way of life. They used this time to really get to know the Mouk people and translate the Bible into their native language. When the missionaries were ready to present the Gospel, they invited the entire village of 310 people to hear the Bible teachings. For three months, the villagers would gather together twice a day. Monday through Friday each session would last about an hour. No one in the village ever missed a session. Even if someone was sick, others would bring them to hear the lesson.

The missionaries used a teaching technique called chronological storytelling. This method walks people through the key points of the Bible in sequential order in a storytelling format. Starting with Old Testament foundational stories, the missionaries taught about God and His greatness, creation, sin, the fall, and man's need for salvation. For two months the Zooks made their way through the Old Testament stories before finally coming to the New Testament. They introduced Jesus as a baby and taught about His life and ministry. The Mouk people fell in love with Jesus and He became their hero. The time came to tell the tribe about Jesus' betrayal, death, burial, and resurrection. Over a series of days, the missionaries taught the villagers about God's great love and Jesus sacrifice. On the final day, the missionaries asked the Mouk people what they believed and many stood and testified about their belief in Christ and the forgiveness of their sins. One after another the tribe people stood and announced their faith in Christ. Mark Zook told the villagers, "If you really are believing what you're saying then God's Word says your sins are forgiven." Everyone in the tribe began to shout, "EE-Taow," which means, "it is true." Then suddenly, spontaneous rejoicing broke out that lasted for 2½ hours. The whole village put their faith and trust in Jesus Christ as their Lord and Savior.

This is an amazing story of the power of God and His Word. I encourage you to do an Internet search using the phrase "EE-Taow" and watch the video yourself. However, there is another reason I bring this up. The missionaries' approach to the Mouk people was ingenious. They used principles and techniques that parents can use in their homes to lead their family.

The Zooks lived in the Mouk village for two years and studied the tribe's culture, language, and learning style. During those two years they were able to get to know the Mouk people so well they discovered and devised a plan to best present Christ to them. As a result, they were able to share the Gospel with the villagers and lead the entire tribe to Christ.

During this week of reading, we are going to explore the techniques of the missionaries and implement the principles they used in discipling our families.

Cultural Pollution Ground Zero

How well do you understand the culture your children live in? As you well know, it is vastly different from the culture you and I grew up in. The 21st century child lives by the word "variety." Children are used to having billions of Internet sites at their fingertips, hundreds of channels on their TV's, dozens of menu items at any drive-thru restaurant, and a vast number of stores at the local mall for shopping. They love variety. Kids in today's culture are accustomed to having numerous choices when it comes to religion. Children see having options regarding spiritual matters as open-minded and socially acceptable. They think that having a smorgasbord of alternatives to God and salvation is something to embrace. Walt Mueller confirmed this idea when he stated,

> In today's postmodern world in which the culture (and many teenagers) wears spirituality on its sleeve, your children will encounter a variety of spiritual options, faith systems, and combinations thereof that seems quite appealing. In addition, our culture's emphasis on pluralism, diversity, and tolerance has created an environment in which different spiritualities aren't seen as mutually exclusive. In fact, our culture sees it as being wise and broad-minded to embrace and combine elements of different spiritualities into your own personal belief system.[2]

This mindset is unbiblical and can often lead to confusion regarding many biblical truths. One example is found in something as simple as salvation. The Bible is clear. Real saving faith is mutually exclusive through Christ and Christ alone. On the other hand, culture would say there are many ways to get to heaven. Children are bombarded by culture from numerous directions and on every level when it comes to the Bible. Therefore, parents have to be ready for the onslaught of misunderstood information that swirls around the 21st century culture and ultimately in their children's mind.

Before parents can be ready to combat the cultural flood of misguided information directed at children pertaining to spiritual matters, they first need to understand where the wrong information originates. A powerful influence in your child's life is the media. Media is a powerful force in a kid's life and unfortunately shapes how they think in many ways. The Internet, TV, movies, and music flood their minds daily with inconsistencies, negativity, and false information regarding religion. Tom McGrath compares several of the mixed signals children receive from the media with respect to the message Jesus proclaims in Figure 1.

Media vs. Jesus

Media would say...	Jesus would say...
You deserve a break today.	Take up your cross and follow me.
Have sex anytime, anywhere, with anyone.	Neither do I condemn you; go and sin no more.
Satisfy every appetite as soon as possible.	Not by bread alone do you live.
Look out for number one.	Seek first the kingdom of God.
Appearance is everything.	Blessed are the pure in heart.
If you're angry, it's OK to be violent.	Turn the other cheek.
Odd people don't belong.	Whoever does the will of my Father is my brother and sister and mother.
Don't acknowledge that a quarter of the world is starving tonight.	Whatever you do to the least of these, you do to me.[3]

Fig. 1. Media vs. Jesus

McGrath points out the vast difference and startling reality of the two viewpoints. It is clear that the media encourages a narcissistic mindset while the Bible promotes an opposite, selfless attitude and way of life. In addition, public education, peers, and cults are also influences impacting current culture when it comes to spiritual matters.

There is an explanation for this problem. Researchers have found why children are so misguided by cultural opinion. The reason comes back to their lack of knowledge regarding biblical truths. Christian Smith discussed this point in detail. Smith interviewed a number of teenagers and found that they lacked "central religious and theological ideas."[4] He stated,

> *When teenagers talked in their interviews about grace, they were usually talking about the television show Will and Grace, not about God's grace. When teenagers discussed honor, they were almost always talking about taking honors courses or making the honor roll at school, very rarely about honoring God with their lives. When teens mentioned being justified, they almost always meant having a reason for doing something behaviorally questionable, not having their relationship with God made right.[5]*

Smith summarized his analysis by saying,

> *In short, our teen interview transcripts reveal clearly that the language that dominates U.S. adolescent interests and thinking about life, including religious and spiritual life, is primarily about personally feeling good and being happy...This, we think, has major implications for religious faiths seriously attempting to pass on the established beliefs and practices of their historical traditions.*[6]

Since teenagers, and younger children as well, do not have a biblically-based point of reference of salvation or other biblical truths for that matter, they are easily captured by cultural ideology.

Based on these findings, the conclusion is simple. Culture and ignorance are to blame for today's tragedy. I know that sounds harsh, but children and teens have been misguided by culture in such a way that they feel they can just pick and choose what seems right to them and determine their own way to heaven. Feelings trump truth. The minds of today's children are flooded by pop culture. Having proper biblical knowledge and basic theological beliefs are seen as antiquated. Kids are inundated by culture's false messages regarding almost every area of the Bible. Parents are left with children who do not have an adequate understanding of the fundamental subjects of God, faith, sin, grace, and Jesus.

There is very little you can do to change culture. However, there are several things you can do to keep culture from changing your family. Study the Bible with your family regularly. Pray with and for them continually. Be involved in a local church that firmly stands on Scripture. Have other godly people in your life and in the lives of your children. Remember: it all starts with you. Keep in mind what James says, "Religion that God our Father accepts as pure and faultless is this: ...to keep oneself from being polluted by the world" (Jas. 1:27).

Home Apps

So you can stay abreast of what can potentially pollute your family, know what Internet sights are popular. Be aware of the TV shows and movies getting the best ratings. Many things kids watch portray the parents as servants, subordinates, or stooges. Don't believe it? Watch a few of the popular shows on the Disney channel or Nickelodeon with that idea in mind and see for yourself. Lastly, music is major. In this area you'll need to do your homework. Find out who the artists are and investigate their backgrounds and current lifestyles. Listen to the songs and read the lyrics as the artist sings the song. Pay attention to their dress and listen carefully to the things they talk about when interviewed by the media. Unfortunately, this is only the tip of the iceberg. However, it will help you better understand where cultural pollution comes from and as a result, ignite a fire and help you realize your need to be a serious student of today's culture.

Day 17

Teach me knowledge and good judgment, for I trust your commands. (Ps. 119:66)

"An investment in knowledge always pays the best interest."
— Ben Franklin

Do you study the culture your children are growing up in?

I had the privilege to be a part of a mission team to the Dominican Republic a few years ago. Our group traveled to three different locations to do daylong Vacation Bible Schools. Two of the three places we did VBS were called batays. The batays were, for a lack of a better word, shantytowns. Most of the people there lived in either blockhouses or grass huts. At best a family of five lived on about $8 to $10 per week. They had very few possessions and made do with what little they had. There was a well at each of the batays that the community would share. For me, a southern boy growing up in North Carolina, it was an eye-opening experience to see people living in such conditions. At the VBS, I was given the chance to teach Bible stories to elementary age children. On the plane to the Dominican, the group leader gave me some VBS material and said, "I want you to use this book and teach these stories the way the material suggests." I agreed and began to study and prepare for the lessons.

On the first day, I had my book ready and did my best to present the lesson. The material was written for the teacher to present the lesson in a small group, classroom setting, in a lecture style format. At each VBS we had over one hundred kids. We divided the kids into groups of about twenty and had them rotate between crafts, recreation, music, and Bible stories. My classes were outside, behind the church building, and under a tree. As I taught each group, I had a very difficult time connecting with the kids. It made our time drag by. The problem was not the kids but me. I knew I was doing a horrible job and boring the kids to tears. I had to make a change.

That night I went to the group leader and asked if I could change up things a bit in my delivery. The subjects the material suggested were great, but I needed to get away from the lecture style the book intended. He agreed. I thought back to the conditions they were living in, what their life must be like in the batays, and how much education they had. I decided to use the same message the material recommended but instead of a sermon I used a storytelling delivery. The next day I was very excited. With my first group, I grabbed two kids from the crowd and made them actors. I had them act out with me the lesson as I taught them in story form. It was a complete success, and we had a great time learning about Jesus raising Lazarus from the dead.

I've always wanted to go back to the first batay and redo the lesson using story form. Maybe one day I'll get to. I had to learn the hard way how to approach my audience, but it taught me a valuable principle about teaching. Always know your audience. Study them and their culture. Know what they're like, what interests them, and, most of all, how they learn. I will never forget the power of using the story-telling method and how well it helped me connect and communicate to the Dominican children.

I know many parents are in the same predicament with discipling their children as I was back in the Dominican. They don't know where to start, how to connect, or how to communicate. Many parents make the mistake of trying to disciple their children the way they themselves best learn. That is not always the best approach. Every child is different in his or her personality, mental capacity, and learning style. What are parents supposed to do? I have good news; the Bible has the answer!

Let's take a look at two obscure people groups found in the Bible to gain some insight as to how we can overcome this problem.

Tribe of Issachar

The tribe of Issachar was a special breed of people. The Bible describes them as, "Men who understood the times and knew what Israel should do" (1 Chr. 12:32). This tribe was known for having the gift of discernment. God had given them the ability to understand the culture in which they lived and to know what they needed to do in order to have success. Parents, consider embracing the Issachar philosophy and study the culture your kids live in. This understanding will enable you to relate to your children. Knowledge of current fads, trends, and events will help you understand how your children think and what influences their attitudes. This can give you valuable information to help make informative and wise decisions for your children and enable you to make God's Word relevant in your child's life.

The Bereans

The Bereans were followers of Christ who lived in the Apostle Paul's day. They were exceptional students of the Word and ferociously studied the Scriptures to understand God's truth. The Bible says in Acts 17:11, "Now the Bereans were of more noble character than the Thessalonians, for they received the message with great eagerness and examined the Scriptures every day to see if what Paul said was true." Perhaps you could adopt the Bereans' tenacity regarding the study of Scripture so you too can know the truth of God's Word.

When parents decide to combine the Issachar and Berean mindsets concerning culture and the truth of Scripture, God can use them in a mighty way. I cannot emphasize enough the importance of personal preparation so you'll be able to make God known to your children. First, be students of culture and its influences on your kids. Second, be great students of God's Word. Third, be students of how each of your children learns…more on that later. In other words, always know your audience. This may not sound practical, but if you'll invest the time in discovering the learning style of each of your children, it has the potential to make a world of difference in their comprehension of the Bible.

Being an Issach-Rean of Today's Culture

Studying the culture can be a difficult assignment for many parents. The world your children are growing up in is very different from the world you experienced. Often parents get left behind or lost in today's culture. Today's music, vocabulary, media, technology and morals have little to no similarity to those just thirty short years ago. These differences easily intimidate parents. However, with God's help you can do this. In order for you to be good students of today's culture, you need to be immersed in what shapes the thinking of today's kids. If you have preschool children, you might think about being more selective of the TV shows and movies you allow your kids to watch. You cannot go wrong in being overprotective in this area. As your children get older, you should be very familiar with the meanings of the words and phrases they use, the music that is popular, the latest blockbuster movie, the bands that are topping the charts, and the latest clothing trends. These can be major influencers in their lives. Unfortunately, it doesn't stop there. If you have older children, you ought to be aware of the latest social media, the hottest videos on the Internet, and the local hangout spots. You should try to be up-to-date on the most popular video games and the popular pop icons. Perhaps one of the biggest areas to consider when it comes to getting inside your child's world is knowing where your kids spend their time, how they use their money (most likely it's your money not theirs), the friends they have, and whom they are dating. You may think I'm going too far on this next one so brace yourself. Get to know the parents of your children's friends. Do they have the same standards that you have? What do they allow in their home that you do not? You're probably thinking, "That's just being too nosy." Okay, then talk to a parent who has older children that are not walking with the Lord and ask them if they would implement any of these suggestions if they had it to do over again. No matter how old your children are, their friends' parents can be either a positive or a negative influence on your kids. Basically, you must be involved in every aspect of your child's world no matter what their age. As a result, you can learn about and understand their culture so that you know what influences them, then steer them in the direction that will honor God. But let me give you one word of warning. Do not make the mistake of trying to fit in with your kid's culture. Do not try to adopt aspects of your child's culture into your own life; it will only backfire on you.

One time on a youth trip, some of my leaders thought it would be funny to make a video of me using the vocabulary and gestures of today's student culture. In the beginning I wasn't sure what they were up to, but I went along with it. It was all clean fun, but I have to be honest, it was difficult and awkward for me. I had a team of teen experts working with me on how to properly enunciate each syllable of every word. They coached me on how to correctly execute each movement of their cultural body language. They had me say about ten different phrases and use several hand gestures into the camera. What should have taken about thirty minutes to an hour to shoot took about three days to record. It was hard work. Once the video was edited and complete, it dawned on me what the video was all about. It wasn't to get the youth pastor to show how cool, hip, and relevant he was to student culture. That wasn't it at all. They simply wanted to make fun of me. They also wanted to send me the message that they didn't want me to use their language because I look stupid when I use it. Needless to say, I got the point.

Media, entertainment, and technology are much different today than they were just ten years ago. However, all these elements have major influences on your child's life. Please don't misunderstand; you don't have to act, dress, and do the same things your children do. However, you should have a grasp of their culture and what influences them. Unfortunately, this takes time, but it is time well spent.

Home Apps

Allow me to suggest some ideas on how to get into their world. Spend some time watching TV shows or movies with your kids. When you're having dinner, start a conversation about the pros and the cons of what you saw. The next time you're in the car with your kids, turn to their favorite radio station. Try listening to their music and discuss the artists and the lyrics of their songs. At bedtime ask them about their day, what they did, and whom they spent their time with. In the mornings before everyone gets started with their day, chat about the latest news event, the hottest new technological toy, or the current fashion trend. When you're purposely aware of these aspects, you will be able to discern the effect they have on your children and better understand how you can relate to them in spiritual matters. Parents must study today's culture so they can properly apply the truths of the Bible to their child's life for tomorrow.

Day 18

Point your kids in the right direction—when they're old they won't be lost. (Prov. 22:6 MSG)

"Aim at nothing and you will hit it every time."
— Zig Ziglar

How do your kids learn best?

It is important to remember the fatherly advice Solomon gave parents regarding their task as the primary disciplers. The Bible says, "Train up a child in the way he should go: and when he is old, he will not depart from it" (Prov. 22:6 KJV). Looking back to Day 3 we discussed the word "train." "Train" in the original Hebrew language is **chanak**. According to David Jeremiah this word has a unique meaning. He said, "An Arab midwife would rub crushed dates on the palate of a baby's mouth to stimulate the instinctive action to suck, so that the child could be nourished. Over time the concept of training up came to mean 'to create a thirst or a hunger within a child for the godly things of life.'"[7] God gives parents the awesome privilege of cultivating a hunger and a thirst in their child's lives regarding spiritual things. How can parents, who are believers in Jesus Christ, help create a spiritual appetite for the Lord in their kids? I don't know many parents who do not desire for their children to have a growing relationship with the Lord. But most parents have no idea where to start, or they give up soon after making a few failed attempts and lose all confidence. It's like trying to hit a target when you don't know where to aim.

Do you remember the Peanuts cartoon? Charles Schultz, creator of Charlie Brown and the gang, was one of the world's best social critics and theologians to every live. For years, the Peanuts cartoon was his platform to make commentary concerning culture and teach biblical truth. One of Schultz's classic cartoons had Charlie Brown at summer camp. He and the other campers were at the archery range. A camper comments on Charlie Brown's incredible ability to hit so many of the bulls-eyes. Charlie Brown says, "Well, I do it a little differently. I first shoot the arrow and then I go and draw a bulls-eye around where it hits."[8] That's one way to build confidence. Drawing bulls-eyes after you shoot your arrow always guarantees hitting the mark. I know a few parents who wish discipleship was that easy. At any rate, the question has to be asked again: how can parents generate a hunger for discipleship in each of their children? How can parents properly aim at the right target and hit it with confidence? The answer, of course, is found in the Bible.

The Bible has all the answers and interestingly enough, the answer is found in the same verse we've been discussing. The phrase translated "in the way" is the Hebrew word **derek**. According to blueletterbible.com the phrase means, "way, road, distance, journey, manner, path, journey, direction, manner, habit, of course of life (fig.), of moral character (fig.)."[9] Chuck Swindoll in his book, *Parenting: From Surviving to Thriving*, gave excellent insight into the word **derek**. He said,

> One visual image associated with **derek** is that of an archer's bow, which has a natural curvature to it… Each child, like a bow, comes with a shape, or a bent, that is natural to him or her. If a bow is to be useful, it cannot remain in its natural, relaxed state. An archer must work with the bow's characteristic curvature, so he can bend the wood in the right direction, and string it so that it might become a source of power.[10]

Not only are parents responsible for producing a hunger and a thirst in their kids, the Bible commands that they create this desire through their natural "bent." John White, of Bible.org, made this statement concerning Proverbs 22:6. He stated,

> *Solomon urges parents to learn well the unique traits of their children. He knew that spiritual training, to be effective, must be "coded" differently for each child so the child will embrace it and, as he or she matures, be shaped by it. Does such an understanding render this great verse toothless? Hardly. What it does is give parents the challenge of their lives—to shape God's truth into a well-aimed arrow that hits the mark deep in the heart of a child![11]*

His commentary sheds a new perspective on the word **derek**. Each child has a unique coding that enables him or her to learn. Parents should consider studying their kid's natural makeup, tendencies, and habits of learning and then customize their discipleship strategy. As primary disciplers, it is so important to discover your child's natural bent as a learner in order to know how to best disciple them.

God has designed every person uniquely, and He loves for people to gain knowledge about Him, the world, and themselves. However, people receive and process information differently. Children and teens gather information in one of three basic ways called learning styles. Educators describe the three learning styles as visual, auditory, and kinesthetic. These different learning styles are explained in detail below:

> *Visual learners process new information by reading, looking at graphics, or watching a demonstration. Children with this learning style can grasp information presented in a chart or graph, but they may grow impatient listening to an explanation.*

> *Auditory learners prefer listening to explanations over reading them and may like to study by reciting information aloud. This type of learner may want to have background music while studying, or they may be distracted by noises and need a quiet space to study.*

> *Kinesthetic learners learn by doing and touching. They may have trouble sitting still while studying, and they are better able to understand information by writing it down or doing hands-on activities.[12]*

The Lord has given each individual a different learning style, or bent, when it comes to receiving and processing information. It has been determined by educators that a child normally learns best by using a blend of the different learning styles; however, one learning style is often preferred over the other two. One thing needs to be clear. Learning is not about how smart a person is. Learning is about the bent God has given a person to use as he learns. The Purpose Associates state, "The learning styles theory implies that how much individuals learn has more to do with whether the educational experience is geared toward their particular style of learning than whether or not they are "smart." In fact, educators should not ask, "Is this student smart?" but rather 'How is this student smart?'"[13] Therefore, a child's bent is vital information for parents to discover. Finding out a child's bent is not rocket science, but a science nonetheless. There are numerous methods accessible on the Internet to aid in this endeavor. Take the time to determine your child's learning style so you can properly implement a discipleship strategy. Learning can be made easier and more valuable when your kid's bent is known and the proper learning technique is utilized. Knowing the unique bent of each child in your home can open up a new world of learning and confidence.

When Victor Seribriakoff was fifteen years old, his teacher told him he would never finish school or amount to anything. The teacher also said that he was a "dunce," should drop out of school, and learn a trade. Victor thought long and hard. Eventually, he decided to take his teacher's advice. Over the next seventeen years he went from job to job aimlessly drifting with no purpose to his life. Since his teacher told him he was a "dunce," he acted like one. At the age of thirty-two years old something amazing happened in Victor's life. He was given a test to measure his Intelligent Quotient. The score revealed he was a genius. Victor Seribriakoff had an IQ of 161! As a result, he started acting like a genius. With his newfound confidence, Victor began writing books, became an inventor, and had a successful career in business.

Home Apps

Do an Internet search using the words, 'learning style quizzes.' You'll find numerous assessments available for free. There are some that require a small fee, but that's your call. Set aside a few minutes to take the quiz and determine your own learning style. Then invite each person in your family to take the quiz. If your children are a little young for quizzes, then it may be a good idea for you to answer the questions with them in mind. This exercise will be valuable to you as a parent to know how each of your children learns best.

Day 19

Careful planning puts you ahead in the long run; hurry and scurry puts you further behind. (Prov. 21:5 MSG)

"Educators have long been aware that learning is not one-size-fits-all. In a typical classroom, some kids process information best by hearing the teacher explain it, some learn by seeing what's on the chalkboard, and others learn through hands-on exercises."
— Emily Graham, of schoolfamily.com

What's your strategy?

The Rumble in the Jungle was one of the greatest and memorable boxing matches in Heavyweight Championship history. On October 30, 1974, Muhammad Ali and George Foreman battled in Kinsasha, Zaire. Ali was known as a technical fighter. He could add up points in a match rapidly in any given round with his finesse and quickness. On the other hand, Foreman was known as "the bruiser." He would approach each fight with two things in mind. Hit hard and make the match as short as possible. The two fighters could not be more different.

As the first round began, no one was surprised when Ali scored several points with his skill and speed. But Ali had a problem; Forman was unfazed. By the end of the first round Ali knew something had to change. With the sound of the bell to begin round two, Ali came out with a new strategy. Foreman came after Ali and began an onslaught of heavy blows and powerful punches. However, Ali held his arms close to his body for protection. As the second round progressed, Foreman began to tire. At opportune times, Ali would also lay against Foreman forcing him to hold up his weight. This too fatigued Foreman. By the fifth round Foreman was drained. Ali's strategy was working. Ali began to land punches with astonishing accuracy to Foreman's head and face. As the eighth round began, Foreman's strength was gone. His punches were weak and unproductive. Muhammad Ali regained his title by knocking George Foreman out in the eighth round. Later in an interview, Howard Cosell asked Ali about his tactic of leaning on the ropes, covering his body with his arms, and absorbing Foreman's punches. Ali called his new strategy the "Rope-a-dope."

Muhammad Ali's brilliant strategy paid off. He was able to use his body to absorb Foreman's hay-maker blows to eventually tire him out and defeat his much stronger opponent. The right strategy works when properly implemented and executed. Do you have a strategy for discipling your children? Believe it or not, just like Ali and Foreman you are in a rumble in the jungle. Your fight is for your children's time, attention, and eternity. But your fight is not with your kid, not by a long shot. It is with the Devil. He wants nothing more than to steal, kill, and destroy you and all your efforts when it comes to discipling your family. Rest assured if you do not have a strategic plan for discipleship in place for your home, Satan will have no trouble causing mayhem and thwarting your attempts of leading your family.

The Lord has placed in every parent's life a special gift. The Bible says, "Children are a heritage from the Lord, offspring a reward from Him" (Ps. 127:3). With this gift comes responsibility. Parents are given the ominous task of being the primary disciplers of the children in their home. King Solomon gave special instructions to parents when he said, "Train up a child in the way he should go: and when he is old, he will not depart from it" (Prov. 22:6 KJV). As the chief disciple-maker, the Lord expects parents to produce a craving in their children for Him as they mature and get older. When you know your child's learning style, you'll be able to help them grow in their relationship with the Lord. Especially during adolescence, God desires parents to cultivate a solid faith foundation in their children. Having a solid foundation will give them the ability to have a long and prosperous life that will be pleasing to the Lord.

To make this foundation solid, it's important to focus on five important aspects of discipleship. Parents have the chance to firmly plant in their kids' lives the desire to know God's Word, to live lives of prayer, to practice spiritual disciplines, to share their faith, and to serve others. Simply put, parents get to teach their children to love God and love others. One way to create a solid foundation is for parents to utilize a biblical tool called "The Discipleship Growth Guide (DG²)." You'll be able to utilize this tool to assist in guiding your child's spiritual growth in these five areas. The DG² is not a discipleship program or Bible study; rather, it is a way the discipler can biblically direct the overall process in the disciple-making effort.

Parents will be able to cultivate these five areas in their children's lives when they sit together, when they walk together, when they go to bed, and when they get up in the morning. While parents spend time with their children, they intentionally make these five areas a natural part of their conversations. As primary disciplers, you'll encourage your kids in these five important aspects to ensure proper spiritual growth. The five areas are:

Bible Reading

Daily Bible reading – A disciple needs to read God's Word every day. The goal is not to get through the Bible but let the Bible get through you. The Bible says, "As I opened my mouth, He gave me the scroll to eat, saying, "Son of man, eat this book that I am giving you. Make a full meal of it!" So I ate it. It tasted so good—just like honey" (Ezek. 3:2 MSG).

Yearly systematic Bible reading – God's Word should be comprehended as a whole not just in part. The Bible says, "Do your best to present yourself to God as one approved, a worker who does not need to be ashamed and who correctly handles the Word of truth" (2 Tim. 2:15).

Scriptural processing – God desires His disciples to not just read the Word but to live it out. The Bible says, "Do not merely listen to the Word, and so deceive yourselves. Do what it says" (Jas. 1:22).

Prayer Time

Daily prayer time – A disciple needs to set aside time during each day to have a conversation with God. The Bible says, "Then Jesus told His disciples a parable to show them that they should always pray and not give up" (Lk. 18:1).

Prayer focus – A disciple should pray with adoration. The Bible says, "Our Father in heaven, hallowed be your name" (Mt. 6:9). A disciple needs to pray and ask for forgiveness. The Bible says, "If we confess our sins, He is faithful and just and will forgive us our sins and purify us from all unrighteousness" (1 Jn. 1:9). A disciple should pray with thanksgiving. The Bible says, "Give thanks to the Lord, for He is good; His love endures forever" (1 Chr. 16:34). A disciple needs to pray for his or her needs. The Bible says, "Give us today our daily bread" (Mt. 6:11). A disciple should pray for others. The Bible says, "pray for each other so that you may be healed" (Jas. 5:16b).

Prayer application – God longs for you to spend significant and quality time with Him. The Bible says, "Let us draw near to God with a sincere heart and with the full assurance that faith brings" (Heb. 10:22).

Spiritual Disciplines

Scripture memorization – A disciple should put God's Word in his or her memory. As a general rule, a person should have at least two verses of Scripture memorized for every year they have been a follower of Christ. The Bible says, "I have hidden your Word in my heart that I might not sin against you" (Ps. 119:11).

Tithing – Believers are commanded to give back to the Lord. You are never more like God than when you give. Giving to your local church a percentage of what He has allowed you to receive is important. It is not about how much a person gives; rather, it is about how much he keeps. The Bible says, "Bring the whole tithe into the storehouse" (Mal. 3:10).

Fasting – Fasting occasionally from entertainment, the Internet, food, or other things helps keep life in perspective. Fasting provides an opportunity to set aside distractions and focus solely on God. The Bible says, "But when you fast, put oil on your head and wash your face, so that it will not be obvious to others that you are fasting, but only to your Father, who is unseen; and your Father, who sees what is done in secret, will reward you" (Mt. 6:17-18).

Witnessing

Pray for the lost – Witnessing begins by praying for the lost. Disciples should be praying specifically for people who do not know the Lord. The Bible says, "Brothers and sisters, my heart's desire and prayer to God for the Israelites is that they may be saved" (Rom. 10:1). Paul's word for prayer literally means to beg. Disciples should beg God for the salvation of their friends, family, and others.

Prepare to lead others – Disciples need to learn how to lead others to Christ. The Bible says, "Always be prepared to give an answer to everyone who asks you to give the reason for the hope that you have" (1 Pet. 3:15).

Talk about God – God expects the disciple to share the good news of the gospel. Disciples can regularly talk about God in their conversations and invite people to discuss spiritual matters. The Bible says, "Go into all the world and preach the gospel to all creation" (Mk. 16:15).

Ministry

Discover their gifts – Disciples need to discover the gifts God has given them. The Bible says, "We have different gifts, according to the grace given to each of us. If your gift is prophesying, then prophesy in accordance with your faith" (Rom. 12:6).

Use their gifts – God has entrusted believers with gifts to serve others. Gifts are not designed to be hidden or to be used selfishly. The Bible says, "Each of you should use whatever gift you have received to serve others" (1 Pet. 4:10).

Focus on love – God has given believers gifts to serve others in love. The Bible says, "Now eagerly desire the greater gifts. And yet I will show you the most excellent way" (1 Cor. 12:31).

Keep in mind that the real goal of discipleship is to become more like Jesus. Discipleship is not something that can be rushed; it is a lifelong process. Take your time. Concentrate on one or two parts of the DG^2 at a time. Remember the elephant illustration from the Day 10 reading? Don't overdo it. Add more elements when you feel your kids are ready. DG^2 is a starting point that gives parents what they need to provide the fundamentals to promote genuine spiritual growth. DG^2 can help you lead your children to pursue Christ daily, be transformed in Christ completely, and surrender to Christ ultimately. When you use some or all of these five important areas in your discipleship efforts, you can confidently know your kids will have a solid foundation as a disciple now and "not depart from it" (Prov. 22:6b KJV) when they get older.

Dr. John Geddie went to Aneityum in 1848 as a missionary. Aneityum is the southernmost island of Vanuatu off the eastern coast of Australia. He had a vision to reach the Aneityum people for Christ. He worked hard sharing the Gospel for twenty-four years. Today, a stone tablet, placed in his honor, is inscribed with these words:

> *When he landed, in 1848, there were no Christians.*
> *When he left, in 1872, there were no heathen.*

It took patience, faithfulness, perseverance, dedication, and focus to accomplish his goal of reaching the people of Aneityum with the truth of the Gospel. He made a difference, but it took time. Will you be willing to do the same to achieve your goals in discipling your kids?

Home Apps

Tonight before everyone goes to bed, gather in someone's bedroom with a pen and paper. Ask each person to give a name of someone they know who does not know the Lord and write their name on the paper. The people on the list could be family members, neighbors, classmates, and co-workers. Then go to the Lord in prayer and beg God for their salvation. (Reference Rom. 10:1)

Day 20

And whatever you do, whether in word or deed, do it all in the name of the Lord Jesus, giving thanks to God the Father through Him. (Col. 3:17)

"Leaders establish the vision for the future and set the strategy for getting there."
— John P. Kotter

Do you know how to get things done?

When Abby and Adam were little, my wife and I would occasionally get treated to a dance fest extravaganza. Our daughter Abby, who was about five at the time, would dress up in her leotard and dance with elegance across the floor while music played softly in the background as we sat in amazement. She would mesmerize her mom and me with her fluid motion and dazzling artistry. Abby, however, was never one to leave her little brother out of the family entertainment. Adam, who was two, would also get into the act. His sister had him join in the presentation as her partner but dressed in a pink tutu. He would come running through the den more like a linebacker than a ballerina. Together they would jump, twirl, and spin across their stage and right into our hearts. By the end of their performance, their mother and I would cheer with laughter and delight. Those were times we'll never forget.

For the longest time I could not figure out how Abby was able to get her brother into that pink tutu so easily. Then it dawned on me. Adam had always been a big ham and loved to have people laugh at him. He enjoyed being the center of attention. Abby understood him and knew how to use it to her advantage. She was a master at getting things done and still is.

How are you at getting things done? Let's take the last few days of reading and put them all together. Now that you understand your child's learning style and know what the Discipleship Growth Guide (DG²) is all about, we can combine the two. Hopefully through today's reading you'll be able to come up with a strategy to help your children grow into solid disciples of Christ. But you have to remember one very important thing. Be selective and don't get overwhelmed with all these ideas. Your job as your child's discipler is for the long haul so take into account that you have to pace yourself!

Visual Bent

For a kid who has a visual bent, parents can easily implement the DG² strategy. A visual learner likes to use pictures, maps, charts, and other visual aids to learn about God and His Word. Also, a child that has a bent toward a visual learning style needs to be able to see the actual passage in the Bible. They have the tendency to remember where certain verses are located on a page. Parents can encourage their kids to set aside time each day to get alone with their Bible and read it for themselves. In addition, parents can recommend that they keep a prayer journal of how God is working in their lives. Memorizing Scripture and learning an evangelistic presentation are not difficult for visually bent kids. These attributes can easily be processed in conversations with children when parents "sit at home and when you walk along the road, when you lie down and when you get up" (Deut. 6:7).

Bible Reading – Children with a visual bent like pictures. Parents can encourage their kids to picture biblical scenes in their minds and imagine what they could have looked like. Parents can help their children visualize the people, the things they were doing, and the items they were using. This will help kids experience the scene in their minds and promote proper learning of the Bible. This process can be used with almost every passage in Scripture. Parents should promote the use of highlighters and note taking when their child studies. It is also important for kids to go to a quiet place when they read the Bible.

Prayer Time – Children with a visual bent are usually organized and like to see things to learn. Parents can encourage their kids to write out their prayers or prayer list. They could prompt them to categorize their lists into logical sections to help them organize their thoughts. As they pray daily, parents should encourage their children to visualize the people and places they have listed. This will help them to connect their hearts to their lists.

Spiritual Disciplines – A child with a visual bent will excel at Scripture memorization. Visual people tend to picture words and remember them well. Parents can have their children write verses on cards and regularly look at them for memorizing purposes. Parents should encourage their kids to break down verses into sections. As they learn each part, they will be able to memorize the verse more easily. If a child does not have an income, parents can let them be the one who puts the offering into the church. If they are employed, parents should encourage them to tithe. Whichever the case, parents should make sure to talk about and show their child the things inside and outside the church the money goes to support. This will help them visualize where the money goes and what it is used for. Parents should also encourage their children to read the verses regarding tithing and fasting. This will help them better understand the importance of these disciplines.

Witnessing – There are a number of witnessing methods and plans of salvation children can learn. Parents can have their kids memorize several of these ways of leading people to Christ. Then parents should help their children imagine witnessing situations and help them role-play encounters. As God gives them the opportunity to share the gospel, kids will be more confident and better prepared.

Ministry – Children who are visually bent thrive in a ministry atmosphere where they can be on the front end of the planning stages of events or activities. Parents should encourage their kids to use their gifts to help with planning or organizing.

Auditory Bent

For children who are more geared with an auditory bent, parents can easily apply the DG^2 strategy. Because these children excel when they can process theology by talking it out, parents need to create an atmosphere in the home that welcomes open discussion. Parents should encourage their kids to participate in Bible study and prayer groups, memorize Scripture, listen to Christian music, and subscribe to podcasts of their favorite Bible teachers. Afterwards, parents can help their children process their discoveries when they "sit at home and when you walk along the road, when you lie down and when you get up" (Deut. 6:7). Kids with an auditory bent make excellent evangelists and servants in ministries.

Bible Reading – Auditory children learn best when they hear information verbally, even if it is their own voice. Parents can have their kids read the Bible out loud daily and listen to podcast sermons or an audio Bible regularly. Each day, parents should set aside time to have discussions with their children on what they are reading. Auditory learners are typically talkative and enjoy discussions to process what they are studying. Parents need to encourage lots of questions from their disciples.

Prayer Time – Children with an auditory bent love to hear their own voice. Parents should encourage their kids to daily pray out loud or sing their prayer to God. At home, parents can have their children pray aloud before a meal and at bedtime. This helps give them confidence when they have opportunities to pray in public. Parents should also encourage their children to make it a habit to verbally praise God, confess their sin, give thanks to the Lord, and personally pray for others. Each day, parents should set aside time to have discussions with their children on what they are praying about to help them process what's going on in their life.

Spiritual Disciplines – A child with an auditory bent is proficient when it comes to memorizing Scripture. Auditory learners do well with memorization when they say a verse out loud or put it to music. Singing Scripture usually comes easily to an auditory learner. This type of learner can excel when he or she uses repetition to memorize. Parents should also teach their auditory learners about other spiritual disciplines such as tithing and fasting. A parent can read and discuss with them passages from the Bible that teach the importance of these subjects.

Witnessing – Auditory children can present the gospel well because of their good oratory skills. When equipped with an easy to remember gospel presentation, an auditory child can be used by God to share the plan of salvation effectively. Parents need to help their kids practice presenting the gospel to give them confidence and make them more proficient.

Ministry – Children who have an auditory bent thrive in ministries that allow them to use their speaking ability. They can be used in a variety of public speaking opportunities inside and outside the church. Parents may need to coach their children through any stage fright they may experience; however, it's worth the effort in the long run. Parents can also encourage their children to volunteer at organizations as greeters, receptionists, and tour guides.

Kinesthetic Bent

Parents with children who have a bent toward kinesthetic learning have their work cut out for them. Fortunately, experts from ldpride.net indicate that only a small portion of individuals have this learning style as their primary bent. However, there are some helpful ways to make implementing the DG² strategy possible. As the primary disciplers, parents can utilize skits, object lessons, and movies to help their students know more about God and His Word. Trips to religious sites or institutions also help in their learning experience. Parents can solidify their child's knowledge by using beats or clapping rhythms to help clarify information and memorize Scripture. The key is making it hands on. It is important that children with a kinesthetic bent be active in evangelism and ministries in their church. As a result, parents can help their kids process their experiences when they "sit at home and when you walk along the road, when you lie down and when you get up" (Deut. 6:7).

Bible Reading – Children with a kinesthetic bent like experiential activities. Parents should try to create an atmosphere that allows hands on discovery of the Scripture. Parents can use objects and props to teach their kids and help them relate to the Bible. Having children act out a story as a parent reads aloud helps them understand the passage on a deeper level. These techniques can be applied in practically every part of Scripture. Parents can also promote the use of highlighters and note taking when their children study the Bible. Parents should be aware that children with a kinesthetic bent need to take frequent breaks when they read their Bible because they often have short attention spans and can easily become distracted.

Prayer Time – Kids with a kinesthetic bent are usually good at imitation. Parents should let their children hear them pray and give them opportunities to pray along with them. Since kinesthetic children have a hard time sitting still, they should change positions frequently or move around when they pray. Parents can help their kids pray more specifically by encouraging them to hold a picture of the people or places they are praying for. Also, prayer walking is a natural activity for children who have a kinesthetic bent.

Spiritual Disciplines – A child with a kinesthetic bent can excel at Scripture memorization as long as he or she is able to be physically active. Parents should encourage these children to use hand motions and props when memorizing verses. Also, activities such as fiddling with objects or being in an unconventional position helps these kids focus. Parents need to be aware that kinesthetic children need frequent breaks when memorizing Scripture. This will reduce their tendency to become distracted. Parents should also allow their kids to give an offering each week at church. Afterwards, parents can to talk to them about the privilege of giving and the reasons why believers give to the church.

Witnessing – Because kinesthetically-bent children are usually good imitators, they can do well with evangelism when they are able to watch a demonstration. Parents need to consider taking their kids witnessing as many times as possible either with the church or as a family. Parents should also take their children on mission trips whenever feasible.

Ministry – Kids who are kinesthetically-bent love to act things out and be physical. It's important that parents encourage their kids to use their gifts in the community and in the church. Parents need to involve their children in the church's drama or creative arts ministries. They can be of great benefit to a church because they tend to gravitate toward expressing themselves through acting things out.

Home Apps

Hopefully by now you've had a chance to discover each of your children's learning style. Based on their natural bent, take the next several days to memorize the Scripture below as a family. Make sure to use the teaching techniques suggested above that correspond to each child's learning style.

"Love the Lord your God with all your heart and with all your soul and with all your mind." (Mt. 22:37)

ENVIRONMENT OF SPIRITUAL GROWTH

Read This First – Week 5 Intro...

Take a deep breath and pat yourself on the back. You've made it through four weeks of enlightening, challenging, and thought-provoking reading, but the journey is not yet complete. We have one more week to work through, and it's possible that the next few days of reading will be the most important ones of all.

This week is about you as a parent cultivating an environment of spiritual growth in your home. Don't let the sound of that frighten you. You are more than capable of getting the job done. The Lord has not gotten you this far just to leave you hanging. Not a chance! You and your family are far too valuable to Him and He's not about to do anything halfway. Each of the previous days' readings have been strategically designed and planned to get you to this point. This week has one specific purpose in mind. The goal is for you to understand how to cultivate an environment in your home that will nurture genuine spiritual growth. There are a number of methods that can be used to encourage spiritual growth in the home. The three unique ways we will concentrate on will be to love God completely, love your spouse sacrificially, and love your children openly. If by chance you already have an environment of spiritual growth in your home, then rest assured the Lord will challenge you this week to take your family to the next level.

Therefore be imitators of God… (Eph. 5:1a NKJV)

"Feelings of worth can flourish only in an atmosphere where individual differences are appreciated, mistakes are tolerated, communication is open, and rules are flexible – the kind of atmosphere that is found in a nurturing family."
– Virginia Satir

Day 21

But if serving the Lord seems undesirable to you, then choose for yourselves this day whom you will serve, whether the gods your ancestors served beyond the Euphrates, or the gods of the Amorites, in whose land you are living. But as for me and my household, we will serve the Lord. (Josh. 24:15)

"I believe the director's primary role is to create an atmosphere where his company can be created."
Charles Keating – British Actor

Ready to roll up your sleeves?

In the beginning God created! He created the heavens, earth, stars, sun, plants, and animals. The Hebrew word used in Genesis 1 for God's handiwork is **bara'**. **Bara'** is used four times in the first chapter alone. The literal translation of **bara'** means to make something out of nothing. John Calvin stated in his commentary, "He (Moses) moreover teaches by the word "created," that what before did not exist was now made; for he has not used the term "**yatsar**," which signifies to frame or forms but "**bara**," which signifies to create. Therefore his meaning is, that the world was made out of nothing."[1] Only God can create this way.

At the culmination of His creation, God created man with a crescendo. The Bible says, "In the image of God He created him; male and female He created them" (Gen. 1:27). Adam and woman were given life. However, God was not finished creating. He brought His image barriers together in a special way. God the Father was the best man of the groom, the Father of the bride, and also the official of the first wedding. Adam and Mrs. Adam were united in marriage and "they became one flesh" (Gen. 2:24b). Thus He created the family. Earth, heaven, marriage, and family are all God's ideas.

Just before Mrs. Adam was created and the family was established, one verse that often gets overlooked describes a very important factor. God placed Adam in the Garden of Eden and gave him special instructions. The Bible says in Genesis 2:15, "The Lord God took the man and put him in the Garden of Eden to work it and take care of it." Adam was in Paradise and first told to "work it." God created Adam to work the garden, not just to sit idly by. Matthew Henry said in his commentary, "The Garden of Eden, though it needed not to be weeded (for thorns and thistles were not yet a nuisance), yet must be dressed and kept. Nature, even in its primitive state, left room for the improvements of art and industry."[2] But there is one more thing to note. God not only told Adam to get to work, He also gave Adam specific instructions to "take care of it" (Gen. 2:15b). The phrase "take care of it" has the meaning of a person keeping, having charge of, and guarding something. Putting these ideas together, God gave the garden to Adam and basically said to him, "I've created you to work this place. I'm giving you the job to nurture an environment that will allow things to grow. I love and believe in you." In comparison with Adam, God calls parents to be nurturers too. Instead of fostering an environment of growth in a garden, He calls parents to cultivate an environment of growth in their home. The Garden of Eden is gone and we'll never be able to work or take care of it, but God has given us another awesome gift. Just as Adam and Mrs. Adam were given the responsibility to cultivate the Garden of Eden, we as parents have been given the responsibility to cultivate an environment of spiritual growth in the home.

How to Begin the Cultivating

An environment of spiritual growth in the home is one of the most important aspects of family life. However, it takes dedication, persistence, and hard work! With that being the case, there is nothing on earth that pays more dividends. The key components in nurturing an environment that will encourage your children to grow spiritually are found in deliberately applying the principles we've covered over the last 20 days.

To this point, our journey has shown how parents are the most influential people in the lives of their children. There are no other people groups that come close, and parents should use this to their advantage. Parental influence is by far one of the most important contributing factors to a positive home environment and for good reason: that's exactly how God designed it. The next important principle we covered revolved around a parent's personal relationship with the Lord. Our thoughts, words, and actions are constantly under a very high-tech surveillance system located inside each of our children. How closely we walk with the Lord can often have a direct affect on our children's personal walk with God. That's why it is vital for parents to draw near to God and surrender their lives to giving their children a hunger and a thirst for the Lord. If parents want to have any chance of cultivating an atmosphere of spiritual growth in their home, this one area cannot be compromised. As parents walk closer with the Lord, they will find three principles of family leadership extremely important in cultivating an environment of spiritual growth. Reading and studying the Bible, praying for and with your children, and making family life a priority can have an enormous impact on the overall environment of the home. When parents earnestly pursue God in these ways, the importance of discovering how to connect with their children becomes more critical. Knowing how your kids learn best can unleash extraordinary possibilities. Unlocking your children's learning styles and implementing the DG[2] strategy can open up a new world of discipleship opportunities. It can help them grow spiritually and become the disciples God desires them to be.

God has designed parents to be leaders of their homes and the cultivators of an environment of spiritual growth. When we as parents seek the counsel of God's Word and make every effort to put Biblical principles into practice within our lives and homes, the Lord can work in astonishing ways. However, sometimes the unexpected happens. What seems like out of nowhere, we notice one of our children who has given his life to Christ pulling away from God. It may be a gradual transformation or an abrupt change, but nonetheless there is a moving away from the Lord. Our hearts break and we agonize as we watch our children drift away from God. As a result, we blame ourselves, feel like a failure, and ask questions like, 'what happened and where did I go wrong?'

One Friday morning, I was with a group of men at a mentoring school in Wilmington, NC. We were in a serious discussion about what it takes today to be a godly man, husband, and father in the home. The conversation led the group to talk about the challenges of creating an environment that would allow spiritual growth to naturally occur on a day-to-day basis. After the meeting, a class member hung around to talk. He told me he and his wife are very dedicated to the Lord and had attempted to raise their five children in the way they should go. As he continued to share about his family his eyes began to water. He said, "I've tried to create an environment of spiritual growth in my home. It's difficult, but my wife and I work hard at it. However, one of my children has drifted away from the Lord. My son is a follower of Christ and he has made Jesus the Lord and Savior of his life. But in recent months he seems to not be as interested in spiritual things. He is spending less time in the Word and has not attended church like he once did. He is grown and out of the house, but I'm still concerned about him." As we talked, I asked this heartbroken father about his other children. Without hesitation he told me about God's grace and goodness in the lives of his other children. He said, "My other children are growing in their walk with the Lord and I only give Him the praise for that." As we kept talking, he asked me a question that I know runs through the minds of almost every parent who has children struggling in their relationships with the Lord. He said, "Where did my wife and I go wrong? What happened to my son?" I looked at the man and asked, "Did you and your wife bring your son up in an environment where you tried to train him up in the way he should go?" He thought for a second and said, "Yes, yes we did." Then I tried to comfort this dad and said, "The Bible says then when he is old he will not depart from it. He'll be back. The Holy Spirit will handle things."

I tell you this story for one reason and one reason only. No family is perfect and every family will go through many highs and lows. Remember: we live in a fallen world and our children have sin natures and minds of their own. No matter how consistent we are in applying any of these Biblical principles, we can still feel like things around us are falling apart. The reality of the situation is that Satan is still running loose in this world and is hard at work in our families. Despite your feelings, bear in mind, there is always hope when you are dealing with God. Recall how we learned from Jochebed to get things done. She put her faith into action, did what she knew to do, and trusted in the Sovereign Lord to do the miraculous. You can do the same. If your child truly belongs to the Lord, then rest assured our heavenly Father will be hot on his trail to get him back. He will always make a way back for any of His children to return when they have drifted, no matter how far they have gone. God actually specializes in second chances. Don't believe me? Just ask Jonah, the Prodigal, or Peter; they are proof.

Spiritual growth can be a reality in your home, but before you begin cultivating an environment where spiritual growth can thrive and flourish, there is one last step to take. Based on the principles we've been studying so far in our journey, there are three final pieces to complete the puzzle. You as a parent must love God completely, love your spouse sacrificially, and love your children openly. On the other hand, perhaps your circumstances are different. The environment in your home is producing spiritual growth. That is fantastic; however, is it time for you and your family to go to the next level of spiritual growth? Whatever the case, if you decide to make improvements in how you cultivate the environment of your home it could change the trajectory of the lives of your children today and possibly your grandchildren in the future. No matter what situation you find yourself in, dig in and allow the Holy Spirit to guide you and your thinking.

I cannot urge you enough to take the next four days of reading and begin to implement a few of these ideas. No matter if you're going at this alone or with a partner, applying these simple ideas has the potential to make a major impact in the environment of your home. Although there are no guarantees, putting these suggestions into practice can increase the chances of developing a healthy environment of spiritual growth. But there is one word of caution: don't try to implement all these ideas at once. Remember it's about persistence not perfection.

Are you willing to do whatever it takes to cultivate an environment in your home that will promote and encourage spiritual growth? Will you make every effort to give your children a hunger and a thirst for the things of God? Will you be a student of your children and understand them well enough to help them develop as a follower of Christ? If you are ready, keep reading and let's get to work because God has created you to work this place. He's given you the job to nurture an environment that will allow things to grow. He loves and believes in you.

Home Apps

While you're driving down the road today, turn off the radio so you can be alone with the Lord. If that's not possible, find some way to have private time with God. Once you've secured your time, pray and ask the Lord for two things. Plead with Him to give you a deeper understanding of His Word. With better knowledge, you'll be able to lead your family in more dynamic ways. Secondly, ask God to show you how to love Him more genuinely. In other words, how you can show your love toward Him. The goal is to love God more completely every day.

Day 22

The Lord your God is one; so love the Lord God with all your passion and prayer and intelligence and energy. (Mk. 12:30 MSG)

"God is ready to assume full responsibility for the life wholly yielded to Him."
— Andrew Murray

Ready for a challenge?

Love God Completely

As we discussed in the first week, just before Moses died, he gave one of the greatest sermons documented in the Bible. In chapter 6 of Deuteronomy, Moses gave explicit instructions to the families of Israel. The Jews know this passage as the Shema. They would recite these verses two times a day in order to keep the ideas of these verses fresh in their minds. Dr. John MacArthur verifies this point when he stated, "The Shema (Deut. 6:4-9; 11:13-21; Num. 15:37-41) was the most familiar Scripture to all Jews."[3]

In the New Testament, Matthew gives evidence that the Shema was alive and well in Jewish culture. Jesus recites a portion of the Shema to a group of religious leaders that were trying to test Him and His authority. Jesus was approached by a group of Pharisees trying to trap Him with a question concerning the greatest commandment. The Bible says in Matthew 22:35-36, "One of them, an expert in the Law of the Old Testament, tested Him with this question: "Teacher, which is the greatest commandment in the Law?"" Jesus brilliantly condensed the whole Law of Moses into two points when He said, "Love the Lord your God with all your heart and with all your soul and with all your mind.' This is the first and greatest commandment. And the second is like it: 'Love your neighbor as yourself'" (Mt. 22:37-39). Once Jesus made this statement, all the Pharisees could do was walk away speechless.

The principles of the Shema apply to every follower of Christ today. That's why it is important that we understand the full meaning of Jesus' words. MacArthur gave his interpretation of this passage when he said,

> The Hebrew word for love in Deuteronomy 6:5 is **aheb,** which refers primarily to love exhibited by the will, mind, and actions rather than love exhibited by feelings or emotions. It is the highest kind of love, for it motivates you to do what is right and noble no matter what you may be feeling. It is akin to the **agape** love of the Greek language, which is the love of intelligence, as opposed to **phileo**, which is the love of emotion, or **eros,** which is physical attraction. The love Jesus speaks of in the greatest commandment is the noblest, purest, and highest form of self-sacrificing love that each person is commanded to have toward God.[4]

When seen through the eyes of the New Testament, every follower of Christ is commanded to have an unrestrained, unadulterated, and surrendered **aheb** love of God. When believers unapologetically have a genuine **aheb** type of love for the Lord, their lives are transformed. With that transformation, the people around them, in particular their family, are the benefactors. When parents love the Lord completely with all his or her heart, soul, and mind, God can give them the ability to cultivate an environment of spiritual growth in the home. That has the potential to leave some people around your house speechless…in a good way.

There are many areas on which we could focus that would make positive changes in the environment of our home, but just for today, we'll direct our attention to three important areas.

Children Should See Their Parents Study the Bible

The old saying, "monkey see, monkey do" certainly applies when it comes to parenting. The children of the home see every move a parent makes. Nothing escapes a child's radar even when he is simultaneously surfing the Internet, texting a friend, and listening to music on his iPod. As a result, kids are quick to mimic all that is done, whether good or bad. Parents have an enormous responsibility to be careful of everything they do. David Jeremiah stated, "Modeling is incredibly important in the process of parenting. We learn far more from what we see in our home than what is said there. Long after our children have forgotten what we have said, they will remember what we do. Images – both negative and positive, pleasant and unpleasant – will be burned into their memories for a lifetime."[5] There are many things a parent can do to help encourage a positive and pleasant image in his child's mind. However, there is nothing more important than the parent letting his or her children see them reading, studying, and memorizing God's Word. This one act has the potential to produce an environment of spiritual growth within the home that could last into the next generation. There is no better way to show love to the Lord and to the family. In Proverbs 8:34-35 the Bible says, "Blessed are those who listen to me, watching daily at my doors, waiting at my doorway. For those who find me find life and receive favor from the Lord." Children need to carry into adulthood the image of their parents giving high priority to Scripture. The results can be life changing for generations.

Parents Should Lead the Family in Worship

Parents, for the most part, find leading their family in worship most intimidating. By and large, parents have not taken leadership as the worship leader of the home. There is seldom any time set aside for the family to gather around God's Word. It is time for parents to step up and be the ones who lead their families in worship. It can be done.

Voddie Baucham in his book, *Family Driven Faith*, asked parents a poignant question about worship in the home. He asked,

> *Why are we here? Does our family exist to prepare children for the Major Leagues? If so, then baseball will be the center of our family's universe, and everything will bow to the whims and wishes of the baseball god. Does our family exist to produce socialites? If so, then our family must revolve around the social calendars of our overloaded teenagers and their hectic schedules. However, if our family exists to glorify and honor God and to lay a Biblical foundation in the lives of our children, then we must not allow anything to interfere with our commitment to family worship, prayer, and Bible study.*[6]

The key is determination. It is up to parents to make family worship a regular reality in the home. No matter where a parent is spiritually, there are countless resources available at any Christian bookstore to help everyone in the family grow spiritually. When parents surrender to the Lord's desires and lovingly lead their family in worship, God can do extraordinary things. Arthur Pink gave evidence of this point when he said, "The advantages and blessings of family worship are incalculable. First, family worship will prevent much sin. It awes the soul, conveys a sense of God's majesty and authority, sets solemn truths before the mind, brings down benefits from God on the home."[7] Therefore, without a doubt, parents need to lead their family in worship. There is no better way for parents to put their love for the Lord on display.

Leading the family in worship does not have to be difficult. There are many opportunities to lead during the week; however, taking advantage of them is the key. Discussing a verse from the Bible at a meal, talking about the latest Sunday school lesson while driving down the road, praying with children before they go to bed, and working on memorizing Scripture together throughout the week are just a few examples. Parents should take advantage of every opportunity to lead their family in worship because each encounter gives your family the chance to draw closer to the Lord.

Parents Should Lead the Family to Worship

Parents have the chance to make it their goal not only to lead in worship but to lead their families to worship as well. All believers are commanded to take part in growing in their faith with other believers. Parents especially should take their families to church and be active participants in church events and ministries. The Bible says, "And let us consider how we may spur one another on toward love and good deeds, not giving up meeting together, as some are in the habit of doing, but encouraging one another—and all the more as you see the Day approaching" (Heb. 10:24-25). However, there is a problem. Where are the men? Many fathers have neglected, even ignored, leading their families to church. As a result, the mothers have picked up where the fathers have left off. More and more, moms are taking the leadership of their family's spiritual growth because the fathers have stepped back from their God-given responsibility. According to Alan Melton and Paul Dean, "In a typical week, mothers are more likely than are fathers to attend church, pray, read the Bible, participate in a small group, attend Sunday school, and volunteer some of their time to help a non-profit organization. The only faith-related activity in which fathers are just as likely as mothers to engage is volunteering to help at a church."[8] This is a sad reality, but dads can do better. Parents, dads especially, should be at the forefront in leading their family in worship at home and at church. Not only should dads get their families to church, they need to get engaged in the events and ministries the church offers and encourage the rest of the family to volunteer as well. Children, especially teenagers, are more than capable of serving in the church. When all is said and done, they just need an example to follow. They need fathers who are in love with the Lord and want to please and honor Him with their leadership of the family.

On the other hand, when the father is not in the picture, for whatever reason, the mother has to take the lead. As you recall, Paul commended Timothy's mother and grandmother for their involvement in leading in his spiritual upbringing. Mom, you are more than capable of leading your family in worship. As a result, expect the Lord to nurture an environment of spiritual growth in your home. Simply put, God may be saying to you today, 'I've created you to love me completely. Your job is to cultivate an environment that will allow things to grow. I'm leaving it in your capable hands to do your part and wait on me to do the rest.'

Home Apps

What do you do if you are the only one in your home excited about making any changes to the weekly routine? What if your children are not even interested? Let me just encourage you to pray and pray hard. You can only do so much, but God can do the miraculous. Do not lose heart and do not give up trying. When your children see your zeal and authenticity it will be noticed and become contagious. What if your spouse is not interested? Of course you need to pray, but let me suggest one other thing. Ask your spouse, or a close friend, if he or she would pray with you about how you can lead your family in and to worship. God can do extraordinary things when we let Him make the moves.

Day 23

A wife of noble character who can find? She is worth far more than rubies. (Prov. 31:10)

"A woman should be home with the children, building that home and making sure there's a secure family atmosphere."
— Mel Gibson

Ready for challenge number two?

An arrogant young boy came to a wise man with a bird cupped in his hands. The boy, wanting to test the man, asked, "Is the bird alive or dead?" The wise man thought for a moment and realized that if he said the bird was alive then the boy could kill it and say, "No, you're wrong." If the wise man said the bird was dead the boy could open his hands and let it fly away, again making him look foolish. After a few minutes of consideration the wise man looked at the boy and said, "I don't know if the bird is alive or dead. But I do know this, the bird is in your hands."

How you treat your spouse is in your hands. Do you show him or her sacrificial love? What does that look like to your spouse? An even better question, what does that look like from your children's perspective? Today's challenge will help you love your spouse in the way God has designed.

Love Your Spouse Sacrificially

Scripture is so incredible. The Bible helps us see how loving your spouse sacrificially has the potential to cultivate an environment where spiritual growth can flourish in the home. Today, as in the Garden of Eden, God unites the husband and the wife and makes them one. There are numerous passages in the Bible that describe the **agape** type of love God expects a husband and wife to share. One of those passages, in particular, is Ephesians chapter 5. When the Lord brings two people together, He gives the man of the relationship very explicit instructions. The Bible says, "Husbands, love your wives, just as Christ loved the church and gave Himself up for her to make her holy, cleansing her by the washing with water through the Word, and to present her to Himself as a radiant church, without stain or wrinkle or any other blemish, but holy and blameless. In this same way, husbands ought to love their wives as their own bodies. He who loves his wife loves himself" (Eph. 5:25-28). On the flip side of the relationship, the Lord gives the woman specific instruction too. The Bible bookends these instructions to the man with two verses for the woman. The Bible says in Ephesians 5:22, "Wives, submit yourselves to your own husbands as you do to the Lord" and follows it up with the command for "The wife must respect her husband" (Eph. 5:33b). Notice the language used in these sets of verses. Words like love, gave, submit, and respect are not accidents. It takes the two sides, the husband and the wife, working unselfishly together to make the relationship work. When parents sacrificially love one another and put these words into practice, an environment of spiritual growth can be a reality. Children need to see healthy, loving, and growing married relationships lived out in front of them. One of the greatest advantages of a healthy marriage is the current effect it has on the children of the home. When children see their parents genuinely loving each other, they feel a sense of security. David Black supports this idea when he says,

> *The relationship between a husband and a wife is the foundation on which children build their sense of security. A child's greatest desire is that his or her parents love each other and thus model Godly love and fidelity. Dads and moms need to covenant before God to remain married, to love each other selflessly, and to allow the love of*

God to permeate their home. The fidelity of our love for one another will transfer to our children, who will, by our example, learn to exhibit fidelity in everything they do. Children need to know that they are loved by both parents and feel the security that parental love provides in an unlovely world.[9]

As a long-term benefit, when parents have a healthy marriage it provides kids with a living example of how to model their own future marriage relationship. There is no stronger message parents can send to their children.

On the other hand, what should a parent do if their relationship with their spouse, or former spouse, is less than ideal? You may be saying, "All that sounds great, but that's not the world I live in. I hope there are people living in that reality, but it's not mine. My spouse (or former spouse) and I don't have that kind of life now. I am all alone." If this is your situation, then allow me to ask one important question. Do you want your children to know how to love someone sacrificially? I mean, certainly you want your children to grow up and have a spouse of their own that they love sacrificially, right? Regardless of how things are between you and your child's other parent, I doubt your answer is anything but "yes." With that in mind, you have to be the one to step up and make sure your children see you loving sacrificially. God calls each of us as Christ followers to love one another unconditionally. That's why Paul reminds us that, "Love must be sincere. Hate what is evil; cling to what is good" (Rom. 12:9).

If there have been hurt feelings between you and your partner, or former partner, then perhaps the Lord is calling you to put an end to the brokenness. At least from your perspective, ask God to forgive you of any wrong words and actions. Then ask your mate or former mate, to do the same. God will forgive you! The other person may or may not forgive you; however, as far as you're concerned, make things right. It's easy to hate someone, especially when you have been hurt. But remember what Jesus lovingly tells us: "Love your enemies and pray for those who persecute you" (Mt. 5:44). If you are a believer, you don't have a choice about love. Besides, your children need to have sacrificial love modeled properly for them today so they can duplicate it in the future. It will help them better understand how to handle relationships. Whether you are married, separated, or divorced, it is up to you to display sacrificial love in ways that honor the Lord and allow an environment of spiritual growth in your home to be cultivated.

There are many practical ways to display love to your spouse. One great way to love your spouse sacrificially is by using positive and affirming words. Warm greetings, expressing sweet sayings, and using the words, "I love you" all communicate feelings from the heart. Children, especially teens, analyze every word and action their parents say and do. Therefore, parents should never talk down or use coarse words to each other. This is particularly true if they are separated or divorced. Parents should never use degrading language or try to put their spouse, or former spouse, down in any way. Instead, parents should use words of encouragement toward the entire family, especially their spouse. They should always try to build up their partners in some way everyday. In 1 Thessalonians

5:11 the Bible says, "Therefore encourage one another and build each other up." Parents should always display positive and nurturing conversation toward each other. Of course, parents will have disagreements from time to time. However, both parents should always strive for an environment of reconciliation, no matter what the cost. This is vital, not only for their marriage now but also for their children's future marriages. Parents need to realize they are modeling for their kids today what their sons or daughters could carry into their own marriage tomorrow. When parents exhibit this attitude, they are putting real love on display that encourages an authentic environment of spiritual growth.

Another way parents can deliberately demonstrate their love is by implementing the 3 D's of marriage.

Dialog daily – Dialog is two-way communication. Contrary to popular belief, in an average day women do not use more words than men. ABC News found that "women spoke 16,215 words a day, while men spoke 15,669. Although women speak slightly more words than men, statistically, the difference is insignificant."[10] Therefore, parents need to put that deception to rest and be good talkers and listeners with their spouse daily. With that in mind, parents should set aside a few minutes each day to have a one-on-one conversation with only each other. That means you may need to tell your children that both mom and dad need some time to talk to each other without any interruptions. Parents should also take time to pray with each other every day. Just before a meal, over the phone, or as you're going to bed take a few minutes to pray about an issue or just pray giving the Lord praise. It's simple, it's easy, and it's bonding.

Date weekly – Every couple needs some time out alone weekly. A meal, movie, or a walk allows time to reconnect and reestablish the relationship without the interruption of anyone else. I know this suggestion can be difficult because of finances for some families. But the last time I checked, taking a walk, sitting on the deck, or cuddling in the bed doesn't cost a penny. Set aside some alone time with your spouse to bond. This pays very big dividends in the long run.

Depart monthly – Getting out of town for an afternoon or overnight has great benefits mentally and physically. Sometimes you just need a change of scenery. When couples take time to get away together, they are able to renew their commitment to each other. If this is difficult because you have young children, maybe you could get a babysitter, take them to a grandparent's house, or bribe a teenager. Whatever you need to do. This renewal allows you to keep the spark alive in your marriage.

Another way to love your spouse sacrificially is to know their love language. What is it you do for your partner that makes him or her feel loved? In other words, know what fills each other's love tank. According to Dr. Gary Chapman, people feel love from another person primarily from one of five different actions. These five love languages are physical touch, acts of service, words of affirmation, receiving gifts, and spending quality time. To get a better understanding of these love languages, you'll need to read the book entitled, *The 5 Love Languages: How to Express Heartfelt Commitment to Your Mate.* Know your spouse's love language and make sure your children see you filling their love tank.

When you show sacrificial love to your spouse, or former spouse, it has the potential to promote an environment of genuine spiritual growth in the home. Simply put, God may be saying to parents today, 'I've created you to love me completely and love your spouse sacrificially. I want you to work hard to cultivate an environment that will allow things to grow. I know you can do it! I'm leaving it in your extraordinary hands.'

Home Apps

I doubt you have time to run out and buy Dr. Chapman's book, read it, and evaluate anyone's love language. However, go online before the day is out and do a search with the description "5 Love Languages Quiz." Take the quiz yourself so you can discover your own love language. I encourage you to read the book and find out what your spouse's love language is. Afterwards discuss what you've learned about yourself with your family at a meal, while you're driving in the car, or at bedtime.

Day 24

One day children were brought to Jesus in the hope that He would lay hands on them and pray over them. The disciples shooed them off. But Jesus intervened: "Let the children alone, don't prevent them from coming to me. God's kingdom is made up of people like these." (Mt. 19:13-15a MSG)

"What a child doesn't receive he can seldom later give."
P.D. James, Time to Be in Earnest

Ready for the third and final challenge? Maybe the most difficult…

Love Your Children Openly

Children are a gift from the Lord. They are strategically and unmistakably placed in the lives of parents. On the day a child is born, the Lord gives the mother and father a mandate to love, nurture, and care for their baby. As the baby grows older, the Lord expects the parents to begin the training of their child in the way he or she should go. This responsibility cannot be taken lightly because there is no one better suited for the job. Alan Melton and Paul Dean list four distinct reasons why God gives parents this important task. They say:

- *There is no one who has the availability to disciple your children like you.*
- *No one else loves your children like you do.*
- *No one naturally knows your children better than you and your spouse.*
- *Most importantly, no one else is commanded by the Lord to disciple your children.*[11]

God has uniquely called each parent to cultivate an environment in the home where spiritual growth can occur and the parent/child relationship can deepen. In order to accomplish these monumental tasks, here are three suggestions to jump-start the process. The parents need to make family mealtime a priority, learn how to talk to their child, affirm their child regularly, and know their child's love language.

Make Family Mealtime a Priority

According to a local survey, 39%[12] of Christian families sit together for dinner 5-7 times per week. In addition, a national survey by *Parade Magazine* said, "One out of four families eats together every night, and an additional 34% do so most evenings."[13] In an article published by Focusonthefamily.com, Jim Burns discussed the importance of families eating meals together and the long-term benefit of investing in this opportunity. He stated, "Children regard your presence as a sign of care and connectedness. Families who eat meals together, play together and build traditions together thrive. Does your family eat together at least four times a week? If so, there is a greater chance your kids will perform better in school and be less likely to exhibit negative behavior."[14] Contrary to popular belief, children need parents in their lives, and an easy way to accomplish this contact is sitting at a dinner table together. For many families today, carving out the time necessary to have a meal together can be difficult. Even though preparing a meal takes planning and preparation, the benefit far outweighs the negative aspects. *Parade Magazine* also added,

> *A recent study from the University of Minnesota reported that teens who had regular meals with their parents had better grades and were less likely to be depressed. From Harvard came word that chances are slimmer—by 15%—that children will be*

overweight if they eat with their families. Researchers at Emory University found that preteens whose parents tell family stories at dinner have higher self-esteem and better peer relations during adolescence....And 12 and 13-year-olds with limited family dinners are a staggering six times more likely to have used marijuana. The study also revealed that 84% of teens said they'd rather eat with their parents than alone.[15]

Time around the table eating a meal together is immeasurable. Parents should count the cost and invest whatever time is necessary to regularly eat together. There is little doubt that an investment of this magnitude has the potential to enhance every relationship between family members. As a result, this action has the potential to produce an environment of spiritual growth within the home that could last into the next generation.

Learn How to Talk to Your Children

Parents will often have to fight with everything they have in order to cultivate an environment of spiritual growth in the home. If parents are going to utilize the benefits associated with eating a meal together, they need to learn how to talk to their children when they have them there. In the book of Proverbs King Solomon said, "The purposes of a person's heart are deep waters, but one who has insight draws them out" (Prov. 20:5). Before parents engage in a conversation with their child it is helpful to remember to talk "with" their child instead of "to" their child. "Communication is not a monologue; it's a dialogue."[16]

In order to have a proper dialogue that will encourage the environment of spiritual growth in the home, parents need to consider these four important areas when talking with their children.

Eye contact – Body language speaks volumes. Parents should never underestimate the importance of looking at their children during their conversation. When parents make eye contact, it communicates more than just words. Looking into their eyes says, "I'm interested in what you're saying." It also helps to reduce confusion, shows respect, and tells them they are important.

Listening – Listening to children can sometimes be a challenge for parents. They may have a different vocabulary that can be hard to decipher. Regardless, parents need to learn their child's vocabulary so they can communicate with them. When parents give their full attention to their children, a child will feel a sense of significance in the eyes of their parents. If parents are reluctant to work on listening skills, it could cost them more than they want to pay and cause unwanted tensions later in their relationship. Christine Field of Lifeway.com states,

When we shut them off, I believe a small door closes in their hearts. If enough of those doors close, soon their hearts will be bolted shut to us when we want them to talk to us and when they most need to talk to us. They'll find someone else to share their life

with. A friend, a girlfriend, a boyfriend. That door will stay closed until they are ready to let us in again – after we have proven ourselves worthy.[17]

Focus – Actions speak louder than words. When parents are having a conversation with their children, it is vitally important to focus on them during the discussion. Parents should stop what they are doing or set aside whatever they are working on and give their kids their full attention. Remember, action speaks volumes to children and sends them the message that they are valued and are worth listening to. This fact is especially true for children during their teenage and adult years.

Careful response – Parents need to be wise in their responses to their children, especially in the area of sin. Parents should never condone any gossip, wrong ideas, crude talk, or sinful behavior. The world looks at sin much differently than the Bible does. However, parents should exercise great caution when they respond to their children. Parents need to make sure that when they speak to their children, they keep their points brief and biblical. The Bible will always have the right answer when addressing any situation. The Bible says in Hebrews 4:12, "For the Word of God is alive and active. Sharper than any double-edged sword, it penetrates even to dividing soul and spirit, joints and marrow; it judges the thoughts and attitudes of the heart." Keeping the lines of communication open between a parent and child cannot be overly emphasized regardless of their stage in life. Wise and loving parents will do whatever it takes to make sure they do their part and know how to make the right connection with their kids and maintain a position of influence in their lives. This extra effort can potentially produce an environment of spiritual growth within the home that could last beyond the next generation.

Affirm Them Regularly

Words are powerful! Words can be used positively or negatively. The Bible says, "The tongue has the power of life and death" (Prov. 18:21a). Dr. Bill Bennett once said, "It was Shakespeare who said, 'Sticks and stones may break my bones, but words will never hurt me.' A statement with this magnitude of falsehood only shows that Shakespeare was not always inspired when he wrote."[18] Because words have such power, parents must be conscious of everything they say to their children, especially during their teenage years. The Bible says, "Do not let any unwholesome talk come out of your mouths, but only what is helpful for building others up according to their needs, that it may benefit those who listen" (Eph. 4:29). James Merritt pleaded with fathers when he said, "Dad, I urge you, be firm with your children and never allow them to use profane or filthy language. And I implore you to set the example by the kind of language you use. I've never done a scientific study, but I'm certain you'd find 98 percent of the teenagers and young people who use foul language heard it first at home."[19] Parents should speak lovingly with encouragement. They should use words that build up their child. In other words, wise parents make sure they watch and weigh every word before they speak it to or in front of their kids. Calvin Coolidge once said, "I have never been hurt by anything I didn't say."[20]

One more and possibly the most significant way parents can affirm their children is by genuinely using three simple words. The words "I love you" have incredible value in a child's life. In a culture devoid of the real meaning of love, children need to authentically hear and feel what real love is. The Bible says in 1 Corinthians 13:13, "And now these three remain: faith, hope and love. But the greatest of these is love." Parents need to exhibit and verbalize love in the home in order to cultivate an environment of spiritual growth. From a larger perspective, saying and meaning the words "I love you" do have immediate consequences. However, these words can also have an eternal consequence. Dr. Bennett stated,

> When a child hears the words, "I love you," or "You are important" come from his earthly father, he is more able to recognize and respond when the same words come from the Father above. If the child only receives silence from the father, then perhaps he assumes that God is silent and unconcerned. If a child hears only belittling words from the father, then perhaps he assumes God is just there to judge and condemn.[21]

Parents should model their lives after the Heavenly Father. Saying and meaning the words "I love you" cannot be more important in a child's life. There are no greater words a parent can use that have the ability to build and enhance the environment of spiritual growth in the home. God may be saying to you today, 'I've created you to love me completely, love your spouse sacrificially, and love your children openly. You can do it! I want you to cultivate an environment that will allow things to grow. Walk with me and we'll do this together. I believe and trust in you.'

Know Their Love Language

In yesterday's reading, we discussed the idea of knowing your spouse's love language. But what about your kids? Do they have a love language? According to Dr. Gary Chapman, your children have a love language all their own. These five love languages are physical touch, acts of service, words of affirmation, receiving gifts, and spending quality time. Discovering which of the five love languages your child has is priceless information. By knowing your children's love language you will be able to know the best way to express your love to them and be able to affirm them in ways you've never imagined. To get a better understanding of these ideas you'll need to read Dr. Chapman's book, *The Five Love Languages of Children*. Know your child's love language and make sure you know how to fill his love tank.

Home Apps

As suggested yesterday, go online and access the "5 Love Languages Quiz." This time let your kids take the quiz. If they are too young for quizzes, try taking it for them and answer the questions the way you think they would respond. The goal is to discover their love language. Also I encourage you to read the book to find out more about your child's love language. Knowing your child better will only bring you closer together as a family.

Day 25

Well done, good and faithful servant! You have been faithful with a few things; I will put you in charge of many things. Come and share your master's happiness! (Mt. 25:21)

"Is it the parents' or the church's job to disciple teens?"
— Steve Wright

How much do you love your family?

A busy mom was at home doing some housework when the phone rang. As she was going to answer it, she stumbled over the loose rug on the floor, tried to grab something to hold onto, but fell across the table the phone was on. The table fell over, made a loud crash, and jarred the receiver off the hook. As the receiver fell to the floor, it hit the family dog. The dog jumped up and ran off howling and barking down the hall knocking over everything in his path. The two-year-old son was taking his afternoon nap but was awakened by all the commotion. Startled by the noise, he began crying and screaming very loudly. The mom, not believing what just happened, rolled over, got herself up on her hands and knees, and dragged herself to the phone. She finally managed to get to the receiver and held it to her ear, just in time to hear her husband say, "Nobody's saying hello, but I have no doubt I have the right phone number."

Family life can be crazy at times; however, nothing on this planet compares to the joy and delight of being part of one. The Lord created this institution and it is His desire for each family to grow physically and spiritually. How's your family doing? Is it growing physically and spiritually? If not, it can. If it is, could there be deeper growth?

One Final Challenge

Scripture is unmistakably clear concerning the parents' primary job when it comes to their children. Deuteronomy 6 and 11 as well as Proverbs 22:6 point to the parents as being the primary disciplers in their child's life. When it comes to disciple-making, parents should reproduce an improved copy of themselves. As it turns out, there is no one better suited for the job, however being a disciple-maker is not an easy task. It takes time, dedication, and a strong conviction. But the most important ingredient to make spiritual growth within the home a reality is having the right environment in the home. According to a study done with over 500 family counselors, Focus on the Family discovered the following top traits of successful families.

- *Communicating and listening*
- *Affirming and supporting family members*
- *Respecting one another*
- *Developing a sense of trust*
- *Sharing time and responsibility*
- *Knowing right from wrong*
- *Having rituals and traditions*
- *Sharing a religious core*
- *Respecting privacy.*[22]

Are some of these traits in the DNA of your home? They can be if you're willing to apply a few of the principles we've studied over the last 24 days. To help in your pursuit of making your home a place where spiritual growth can occur, let me offer a few more suggestions...actually, more like 52 suggestions or one per week. Carefully consider implementing the following ideas:

1. Have a game night with the family (cards or board games not video games).
2. Eat dinner together with no TV for seven consecutive days.
3. Read the Bible together every night before bed for a whole month.
4. Sit together as a family during the worship service at your church.
5. Turn off the TV for one night during the week.
6. Dads take your daughters and moms take your sons out for a lunch or coffee date.
7. Dads, open doors for your wife at home and out in the community.
8. Go for a walk together as a family.
9. Make every effort to be at every extracurricular event your kids participate in.
10. Go on a picnic together as a family.
11. Ask God to bless your food at every meal.
12. Have lots of pictures on the walls, tables, and shelves of your family (not made at a studio).
13. Put a puzzle together.
14. Watch a sporting event on TV or go to a sporting event together.
15. Pick a night of the week for the next several weeks to be "favorite meal night." Each family member gets a turn to choose the menu.
16. Share stories about the things you did while you dated.
17. Go on a short-term mission trip together.
18. Do not talk on the cell phone when you have your children in the car with you.
19. Help your children with their homework.
20. Be involved in the ministries at your church your kids are in.
21. Go on field trips with your kids.
22. Have breakfast for dinner one night.
23. Sit out under the stars at night.
24. Make homemade ice cream.
25. Go out and buy squirt guns, marshmallow guns, air soft guns, or, if you like living on the edge, paint ball guns for each member of the family. Divide the family into two teams and have an all out war.
26. Say "yes" to your child when they ask you to play.
27. Play charades as a family, but only use subjects from your family's past experiences together.
28. Plant a garden together.
29. Establish some traditions during special times of the year.
30. Spend an evening looking at past photos.
31. Learn how to play your kid's computer or video games and challenge them to a game.

32. Do a community service project together.
33. Wash the family pet together.
34. Support a child in a third world country as a family.
35. Go out and buy a box of doughnuts.
36. Make sure bedtime is a happy time.
37. Celebrate together when someone from the family returns home from a short trip.
38. Let one of your children lead in a family devotion time.
39. Have a pizza and movie night.
40. Eat lunch at school with your children.
41. Have family group hugs.
42. Kiss everyone when leaving the house.
43. Dad, have a sleepover in the basement (or den) with the kids.
44. Sing with the radio while children are riding with you in the car.
45. Have a backyard campfire with the entire family.
46. Bake cookies together as a family.
47. Have one person wash the dishes, another dry, and someone else put the dishes away after a meal. While you're working, talk about the last big family event you had together. This could have been a reunion, vacation, or church event. The goal is to find out what made it special for everyone.
48. Do yard work together.
49. Wave goodbye from the front door as someone leaves the house.
50. Take a family walk.
51. Lie down with your children on the floor, on a bed, or outside in the grass. Show them how to "be still" and think about God.
52. Go fishing or camping as a family.

Are any of these suggestions do-able? Most of these ideas will not cost you anything except time. Hopefully this list will help you begin or continue to grow a positive disciple-making environment within your home.

Let me close by asking you to go back and remember the verse we discussed on day 15 from Joshua 24. Joshua said, "But as for me and my household, we will serve the Lord" (Josh. 24:15b). These words can give great hope and encouragement when applied in the home. However, there is a second part of the story that needs to be mentioned. If you turn just a few pages from that verse to the next book of the Bible, you'll find a passage that will make you stop and seriously think about your focus as a parent. Judges 2:8-10 says,

> *Joshua son of Nun, the servant of the LORD, died at the age of a hundred and ten. And they buried him in the land of his inheritance, at Timnath Heres in the hill country of Ephraim, north of Mount Gaash. After that whole generation had been gathered*

to their ancestors, another generation grew up who knew neither the LORD nor what he had done for Israel.

In other words, the generation that came after Joshua did not follow God. What a sad legacy. Could this have been avoided? Did Joshua do everything he ought to have done as a leader, as a parent? Perhaps he needed to be more assertive as the one in charge of a nation regarding parental responsibilities. Maybe he should have gone on an "as for me and my house" Israeli tour to train parents how to parent. There are numerous questions to ask and countless speculations to make that would only lead to more questions and more speculations. Nevertheless, the fact remains; Joshua and his contemporaries failed to pass the baton of faith to the next generation. The bottom line is that you, your family, or the next generations do not have to experience this fate. Do you want to one day hear, "Well done, good and faithful servant" (Mt. 25:21a)? You can if you will humbly come before the Lord and:

- *Take full advantage of the fact that you are the most influential person in your children's lives.*
- *Daily deepen your relationship with the Lord and seek Him with all your heart, soul, mind, and strength.*
- *Consistently strive to be the spiritual leader of your family and show them the way into the presence of the Lord through prayer and study of the Word.*
- *Become a student of your children and their culture so you can know best how to train them as Christ followers.*
- *Do whatever is necessary to provide an environment of spiritual growth in your home.*

Accept these challenges. Put God's Word to the test. Apply His principles to your life. Relentlessly pursue Christ. Trust the Lord. Then one day you'll stop and see your children experiencing a much deeper walk with the Lord that far exceeds your own. Isn't that the goal? What are you waiting for? You can do this…

Home Apps

At dinner or at bedtime tonight ask each member of your family this one question. "How do you know I love you?" Let them know the importance of being open and honest with you. Assure them you only want to make the environment of your home better. Ask them not to pull any punches. Once you've asked the question, brace yourself but know that whatever their response is, it can only help make your home a better place to live and grow.

Appendix

During an average week, how many days do you read your Bible?

	Mom	% Mom	Dad	% Dad	%
Never	1	4%	0	0%	2%
1-2 times per week	9	39%	7	33%	36%
3-4 times per week	5	22%	7	33%	27%
5-7 times per week	8	35%	7	33%	34%

Who typically leads the family devotion time?

	Mom	% Mom	Dad	% Dad	%
Dad	7	30%	8	38%	34%
Mom	4	17%	2	10%	14%
Child	0	0%	0	0%	0%
We Alternate	0	0%	3	14%	7%
We don't do family devotion time	12	52%	8	38%	45%

During an average week, how many days do you specifically pray for your child(ren)?

	Mom	% Mom	Dad	% Dad	%
Never	1	4%	1	5%	5%
1-2 times per week	2	9%	2	10%	9%
3-4 times per week	4	17%	4	19%	18%
5-7 times per week	16	70%	14	67%	68%

During an average week at home, how many times does your family sit together and eat dinner at the kitchen or dining room table?

	Mom	Dad	%
Never	1	0	2%
1-2 times per week	2	5	16%
3-4 times per week	12	7	43%
5-7 times per week	8	9	39%

Endnotes

Tag You're It – Chapter 1

[1] Steve Wright and Chris Graves, *ApParent Privilege: That the next generation might know… Psalm 78:6* (Wake Forest, NC: InQuest Publishing, 2008), 18.

[2] Ibid., 18.

[3] David Alan Black, *The Myth of Adolescence: Raising Responsible Children in an Irresponsible Society* (Yorba Linda, CA: Davidson Press, 1999), 41.

[4] Ken Hemphill and Richard Ross, *Parenting with Kingdom Purpose* (Nashville, TN: B&H Publishing, 2005), 50.

[5] Ibid., 50.

[6] Reggie Joiner and Casey Nieuwhof, *Parenting Beyond Your Capacity: Connect Your Family to a Wider Community* (Colorado Springs, CO: David C. Cook, 2010), 27.

[7] Christian Smith, and Melinda Lundquist Denton, *Soul Searching: The Religious and Spiritual Lives of American Teenagers* (New York, NY: Oxford University Press, 2005), 261.

[8] Steve Wright and Chris Graves, *Rethink: Decide for Yourself, Is Student Ministry Working?* (Wake Forest, NC: InQuest Publishing, 2008), 48.

[9] Ibid., 48-49.

[10] Alan Melton and Paul Dean, *Disciple Like Jesus for Parents: Following Jesus' Method and Enjoying the Blessings of Children* (n.p.: Xulon Press, 2009), 59-60.

[11] David Jeremiah, *Hopeful Parenting: Encouragement for Raising Kids Who Love God* (Colorado Springs, CO: David C. Cook, 2008), 71.

[12] Ibid., 71-72.

[13] Ken Ham and Britt Beemer, *Already Gone: Why Your Kids Will Quit Church and What You Can Do To Stop It* (Green Forest, AR: Master Books, 2009), 32.

[14] Richard Swenson, *Margin: Restoring Emotional, Physical, Financial, and Time Reserves to Overloaded Lives* (Colorado Springs, CO: Navpress, 2004), 122.

[15] Paul Renfro, Brandon Shields, and Jay Strother, *Perspectives on Family Ministry: 3 Views* (Nashville, TN: B&H Publishing, 2009), 25.

[16] Steve Wright and Chris Graves, *Rethink: Decide for Yourself, Is Student Ministry Working?* (Wake Forest, NC: InQuest Publishing, 2008), 86.

[17] Ibid., 150.

[18] Ibid., 106.

[19] George Barna, *Revolutionary Parenting: What the Research Shows Really Works* (Carol Stream, IL: Tyndale House Publishers, 2007), 106.

[20] Reggie Joiner and Casey Nieuwhof, *Parenting Beyond Your Capacity: Connect Your Family to a Wider Community* (Colorado Springs, CO: David C. Cook, 2010), 64.

[21] Ibid.,72.

[22] Mark Kelly, "Parents and Churches Can Help Teens Stay in Church," *Lifeway*, available from: http://www.lifeway.com/article/165963, accessed January 12, 2011.

[23] Ibid.

Chapter 2 – It All Starts with You

[1] Steve Wright and Chris Graves. *Rethink: Decide for Yourself, Is Student Ministry Working?* (Wake Forest, NC: InQuest Ministries, 2008), 82.

[2] Ibid., 82.

[3] John Maxwell, *The 21 Irrefutable Laws of Leadership* (Nashville, TN: Thomas Nelson Publishing, 1998), 136.

[4] Michelle Anthony, *Spiritual Parenting: An Awakening for Today's Families* (Colorado Springs, CO: David C. Cook, 2010), 142.

[5] Ken Hemphill and Richard Ross, *Parenting with Kingdom Purpose* (Nashville, TN: B & H Publishing Group, 2010), 36.

[6] Mark Kelly, "Lifeway Research: Parents, Churches Can Help Teens Stay in Church," *Lifeway*, available from: http://www.lifeway.com/article/165950/, accessed January 13, 2011.

[7] Norma Schmidt, "Being What We Want to See: What a Bag of Peaches Taught Me About Parenting," *Ezine@rticles*, available from: http://ezinearticles.com/119226, accessed January 15, 2011.

[8] John Maxwell, *The 21 Irrefutable Laws of Leadership* (Nashville, TN: Thomas Nelson Publishing, 1998), 138.

[9] Christian Smith, and Melinda Lundquist Denton, *Soul Searching: The Religious and Spiritual Lives of American Teenagers* (New York, NY: Oxford University Press, 2005), 57.

[10] David Roach, "Waggoner Finds American Protestants Deviate from Biblical Discipleship Standards," *Lifeway,* available from: http://www.lifeway.com/ article/169247, accessed January 16, 2011.

[11] See Appendix.

[12] David Roach, "Waggoner Finds American Protestants Deviate from Biblical Discipleship Standards," *Lifeway*, available from: http://www.lifeway.com/ article/169247, accessed January 16, 2011.

[13] John Maxwell, *Leadership Promises for Every Day* (Nashville, TN: Thomas Nelson Publishing, 2003), 388.

[14] Unknown Author, "Quotes," *thinkexist*, available from: http://www.thinkexist.com, accessed on August 1, 2011.

[15] Norma Schmidt, "Being What We Want to See: What a Bag of Peaches Taught Me About Parenting," *Ezine@rticles*, available from: http://ezinearticles.com/119226, accessed January 15, 2011.

[16] John Maxwell, *The 21 Irrefutable Laws of Leadership* (Nashville, TN: Thomas Nelson Publishing, 1998), 138.

[17] William Barclay, *The New Daily Study Bible: The Letters to the Philippians, Colossians, and Thessalonians* (Louisville, KY: Westminster John Knox Press, 2003), 185-186.

[18] Bill Hybels, "Vision," *Sermon Illustrations*, available from: http://www.sermonillustrations.com/a-z/v/vision.htm, accessed August 1, 2011.

[19] John Maxwell, http://www.stpaulwestlake.org/PDF/casting_vision.pdf, accessed August 1, 2011.

[20] Bits & Pieces, "Success," *Sermon Illustrations*, available from: http://www.sermonillustrations.com/a-z/s/success.htm, accessed January 15, 2012.

Chapter 3 – Spiritual Leadership in the Home

[1] John Maxwell, *The 21 Irrefutable Laws of Leadership* (Nashville, TN: Thomas Nelson Publishing, 1998), 138.

[2] David Black, *The Myth of Adolescence* (Yorba Linda, CA: Davidson Press, 1999), 50.

[3] Jim Burns, *Confident Parenting* (Bloomington, IL: Bethany House Publishers, 2007), 59.

[4] Ken Ham and Steve Ham, *Raising Godly Children in an Ungodly World: Leaving a Lasting Legacy* (Green Forest, AR: Master Books, 2009), 108.

[5] See Appendix.

[6] Christian Smith, and Melinda Lundquist Denton, *Soul Searching: The Religious and Spiritual Lives of American Teenagers* (New York, NY: Oxford University Press, 2005), 56.

[7] Ron Luce, *Re-Create: Building a Culture In Your Home Stronger Than The Culture Deceiving Your Kids* (Ventura, CA: Regal, 2008), 134.

[8] R. Kent Hughes, *Luke: Volume 1* (Wheaton, IL: Crossway Books, 1998), 100.

[9] James Merritt, *In a World of...Friends, Foes, and Fools: Fathers Can Teach Their Kids to Know the Difference* (n.p.: Xulon Press, 2008), 194.

[10] See Appendix.

[11] Ibid.

[12] Patrick M. Morley, *The Man in the Mirror* (Nashville, TN: Thomas Nelson, 1992), 126-127.

[13] Sparky Anderson, *Brainyquotes*, available from: http://www.brainyquote.com/quotes / quotes/s/sparkyande139386.html, accessed on March 14, 2012.

[14] Rod Cooper, "Being the Leader God Wants You to Be: Finding Honor and Respect at Home" (sermon, Lakeview Baptist Church, Hickory, NC, September 8, 2006).

[15] Ibid.

[16] Ibid.

[17] Ibid.

[18] Ibid.

[19] Ibid.

[20] Bobby Bowden, "Bobby Bowden's Talk" (lecture, Hickory Metro Convention Center, Hickory, NC, December 6, 2010).

[21] Ibid.

[22] Ibid.

[23] Ibid.

Chapter 4 – A Different Approach

[1] James Merritt. Interview by author, Cross Pointe Church, Duluth, GA, September 28, 2010.

[2] Walt Mueller, *The Space Between: A Parent's Guide to Teenage Development* (Grand Rapids, MI: Zondervan 2009), 84.

[3] Tom McGrath, *Raising Faith-Filled Kids: Ordinary Opportunities to Nurture Spirituality at Home* (Chicago, IL: Loyola Press, 2000), 238.

[4] Christian Smith and Melinda Lundquist Denton, *Soul Searching: The Religious and Spiritual Lives of American Teenagers* (New York, NY: Oxford University Press, 2005), 167.

[5] Ibid., 167-168.

[6] Ibid., 168.

[7] David Jeremiah, *Hopeful Parenting: Encouragement for Raising Kids Who Love God* (Colorado Springs, CO: David C. Cook, 2008), 72.

[8] Dean O'bryan, "It's His Church," *Sermon Central*, available from: http://www. sermoncentral. com/sermons/its-his-church-dean-obryan-sermon-on-church-purpose-of-51707.asp, accessed on March 15, 2012.

[9] *Blue Letter Bible*, "Dictionary and Word Search for derek (Strong's 1870)," Blue Letter Bible, available from: http://www.blueletterbible.org/ lang/lexicon/lexicon.cfm? Strongs=H1870&t=NIV, accessed February 20, 2011.

[10] Chuck Swindoll, *Parenting: From Surviving to Thriving* (Nashville, TN: Thomas Nelson Publishing, 2006), 24.

[11] John White, "The Way He Should Go," *Bible.org*, available from: http://bible.org/ illustration/proverbs-226, accessed February 20, 2011.

[12] Emily Graham, "What Is Your Child's Learning Style?" *School Family.com*, available from: http://www.schoolfamily.com/school-family-articles/article/826-what-is-your-childs-learning-style, accessed February 20, 2010.

[13] The Purpose Associates, "Learning Styles," *Funderstanding*, available from: http://www. funderstanding.com/content/learning-styles, accessed December 14, 2010.

Chapter 5 – Environment of Spiritual Growth

[1] John Calvin, "Commentary on Genesis: Chapter 1," *Blue Letter Bible*, available from: http://www.blueletterbible.org/commentaries/comm _view.cfm? AuthorID=5&contentID=3169&commInfo=13&topic=Genesis&ar=Gen_1_1, accessed on February 22, 2011.

[2] Matthew Henry, "Commentary on Genesis 2," *Blue Letter Bible*, available from: http://www.blueletterbible.org/commentaries/comm_view.cfm?AuthorID=4& contentID =629&commInfo =5&topic=Genesis&ar=Gen_2_15, accessed February 23, 2011.

[3] John MacArthur, "Jesus Silences His Critics: The Great Commandment," *Bible Bulletin Board*, available from: http://www.biblebb.com/files/mac/sg2358.htm, accessed December 14, 2010.

[4] Ibid.

[5] David Jeremiah, *Hopeful Parenting: Encouragement for Raising Kids Who Love God* (Colorado Springs, CO: David C. Cook, 2008), 155-156.

[6] Voddie Baucham, *Family Driven Faith: Doing What it Takes to Raise Sons and Daughters Who Walk with God* (Wheaton, IL: Crossway Books, 2007), 137-138.

[7] Ibid., 143.

[8] Alan Melton and Paul Dean, *Disciple Like Jesus For Parents: Following Jesus' Method and Enjoying the Blessings of Children* (n.p.: Xulon Press, 2009), 77.

[9] David Alan Black, *The Myth of Adolescence: Raising Responsible Children in an Irresponsible Society* (Yorba Linda, CA: Davidson Press, 1999), 35.

[10] Ashley Phillips, "Study:Women Don't Talk More Than Men," *ABC News,* available from: http://abcnews.go.com/Technology/story?id=3348076&page=1, accessed March 8, 2011.

[11] Alan Melton and Paul Dean, *Disciple Like Jesus For Parents: Following Jesus' Method and Enjoying the Blessings of Children* (n.p.: Xulon Press, 2009), 59-60.

[12] See Appendix.

[13] Mark Clements Research, "The Truth About Family Dinners," *Parade*, available from: http://www.parade.com/articles/editions/2007/edition_11-11-2007/Family_Dinners, accessed February 12, 2011.

[14] Jim Burns, "Family Time and Relationships," *Focus On the Family*, available from: http://www.focusonthefamily.com/parenting/building_relationships/celebrating_ your_family_identity.aspx, accessed March 7, 2011.

[15] Mark Clements Research, "The Truth About Family Dinners," *Parade*, available from: http://www.parade.com/articles/editions/2007/edition_11-11-2007/Family_Dinners, accessed February 20, 2011.

[16] Ginger Plowman, "Talking So Your Children will Listen," *Lifeway*, available from: http://www.lifeway.com/article/166936/, accessed March 7, 2011.

[17] Christine Field, "If We Listen, Special Needs Homeschooling," *homeschoolblogger.com*, available from: http://homeschoolblogger.com/hsbcompanyblog/126877/, accessed March 7, 2011.

[18] Bill Bennett, *Don't Be a Dude, Be a Dad* (n.p.:n.d.), 4.

[19] James Merritt, *In a World of…Friends, Foes, and Fools: Fathers Can Teach Their Kids to Know the Difference* (n.p.: Xulon Press, 2008), 46.

[20] Ibid., 37.

[21] Bill Bennett, *Don't Be a Dude, Be a Dad* (n.p.:n.d.), 5.

[22] Focus on the Family Bulletin, "Family," *Sermon Illustrations*, available from: http://www.sermonillustrations.com/a-z/f/family.htm, accessed January 15, 2012.

Recommended Reading List

David Jeremiah, *Hopeful Parenting: Encouragement for Raising Kids Who Love God* (Colorado Springs, CO: David C. Cook, 2008).

Chuck Swindoll, *Parenting: From Surviving to Thriving* (Nashville, TN: Thomas Nelson Publishing, 2006).

James Merritt, *In a World of...Friends, Foes, and Fools: Fathers Can Teach Their Kids to Know the Difference* (n.p.: Xulon Press, 2008).

Ron Luce, *Re-Create: Building a Culture In Your Home Stronger Than The Culture Deceiving Your Kids* (Ventura, CA: Regal, 2008).

Ken Hemphill and Richard Ross, *Parenting with Kingdom Purpose* (Nashville, TN: B & H Publishing Group, 2010).

Michelle Anthony, *Spiritual Parenting: An Awakening for Today's Families* (Colorado Springs, CO: David C. Cook, 2010).

Richard Swenson, *Margin: Restoring Emotional, Physical, Financial, and Time Reserves to Overloaded Lives* (Colorado Springs, CO: Navpress, 2004).

Reggie Joiner and Casey Nieuwhof, *Parenting Beyond Your Capacity: Connect Your Family to a Wider Community* (Colorado Springs, CO: David C. Cook, 2010).

Steve Wright and Chris Graves, *ApParent Privilege: That the next generation might know... Psalm 78:6* (Wake Forest, NC: InQuest Publishing, 2008).

Mark A. Holmen, *Building Faith at Home: Why Faith at Home Must Be Your Church's #1 Priority* (Ventura, CA: Regal Books, 2007).

Mark A. Holmen, *Impress Faith on Your Kids* (Nashville, TN: Randall House, 2011).

Doug and Lisa Cherry, *Stick: Making the Handoff to the Next Generation* (Carbondale, IL: Frontline Family Ministries, 2011).

Gary Chapman, *The Five Love Languages of Children* (Chicago, IL: Northfield Publishing, 1997).

Gary Chapman, *The Five Love Languages of Teenagers* (Chicago, IL: Northfield Publishing, 2000).

Alan Melton and Paul Dean, *Disciple Like Jesus For Parents: Following Jesus' Method and Enjoying the Blessings of Children* (n.p.: Xulon Press, 2009).

About the Author

Mark Smith and his high school sweetheart, Sherri, have been married since 1987. The Lord has blessed them with two wonderful children: Abby and Adam. He has served in student ministry for over twenty years and is currently student pastor at Lakeview Baptist Church in Hickory, North Carolina. Mark graduated from North Carolina State University in engineering, Southeastern Baptist Theological Seminary with a Master of Divinity, and Liberty Baptist Theological Seminary with a Doctorate of Ministry.

CPSIA information can be obtained at www.ICGtesting.com
Printed in the USA
BVOW060715300712

296504BV00004B/1/P